# The Key To Auto Shop Marketing

*Your Personal Guide to Skyrocket Your Car Count*

Jonathan Barber

The Key To Auto Shop Marketing
*Your Personal Guide to Skyrocket Your Car Count*


Jonathan Barber
jonathan@socialleafmarketing.com

Printed in the United States of America
First Printing 2019
First Edition 2019

10 9 8 7 6 5 4 3 2 1

# The Key To
# Auto Shop Marketing

# Endorsements

"Exactly what I was looking for. Jonathan positions marketing in a light that just makes sense to auto shop owners."

**Refugio Davila Owner of Davila Auto Service**

"Not your generic marketing book. This book is specifically written for auto shops. I've managed to skyrocket my car count so I'm busy even during my usually slow season."

**Donny Suh General Manager at D1 Auto Body Shop**

"This book just flat out makes sense to me. Nobody else to my knowledge has covered this subject as in depth as Jonathan. Highly suggested read if you want to improve your marketing yourself."

**Bob Tun Owner at Nash Auto Center**

# Table of Contents

# Introduction

*For you, the auto shop owner...*

As an auto shop owner, you're familiar with the *complexity* of a machine.

You deal with systems and moving parts all day long.

Though the cars you repair vary by make, model, and year, they are all governed by the same, general principles.

Online marketing is no different; it is also a system with moving parts, and the most profitable marketing systems to date share a common core framework of governing principles.

This book will reveal that precise, core framework.

The purpose of this book is to reveal and teach the framework and principles of online marketing (reaching, engaging, and turning leads into paying customers) to help auto shop owners and managers attract more customers and accelerate profits and growth.

I recognize the term "online marketing" might be initially intimidating. Don't worry. As an auto shop professional, you already have a systems-oriented mind, and it will not be hard for you to learn.

So, don't let marketing technology intimidate you. I have positioned the subject matter in this book so it is highly relatable to system-oriented minds like yours.

## How to Read this "Manual"

If you read this book from start to finish, I promise you will be in a great position to begin capitalizing on today's marketing technology to capture and convert sales leads. To that end, don't skip any pages. Each section is made up of powerful and detailed steps needed to develop your marketing strategy.

I've also designed this book so that it covers the most important marketing areas first so you can begin applying principles and get your marketing vehicle into gear as soon as possible.

Each chapter generally contains the following information:

1. Topic Overview
2. Why it's Important
3. How it Works (and recommended tools)
4. What's Next

## Marketing System Overview

Every shop needs an effective marketing system built on a sound marketing strategy. To teach what constitutes "effective marketing," this book is divided into three parts. To explain them, here's an analogy you are no doubt very familiar with. As you know, a car has three essential systems:

- Power source: including ignition, electrical, fuel, and engine.
- Power regulation controls: including cooling, lubrication, exhaust, and brake.

- Drive train: including transmission, steering, and suspension.

Effective marketing systems have those same essential systems.

## Your Marketing Power Sources

In my experience, these are the three most important marketing power sources for turning a maximum profit:

### *Power Source #1: Reputation*

Your number one profit "power source" is your *reputation.* You can bedazzle your market with cool promotional material, a great website, and killer discounts, but people won't hand over their time and money "power" if they don't trust you. The only way they can trust you is if they've heard good things about you through reviews, testimonials, etc.

These days, in order to see reviews and testimonials, customer prospects must be able to find you online. I will be covering those topics and many more in this book. For now, remember this:

*Your reputation is a primary power source.*

**_Power Source #2: Investment Mindset_**

If you want to grow your business as quickly as possible and generate high-quality leads, it's important to adopt as an "**investment mindset.**"

Many automotive shops refuse to invest 5% to 7% of their gross revenue back into their business, then they wonder why their business isn't growing quickly. Don't be like those shops. When you wisely invest money into an effective marketing strategy, your revenue will not run dry; it will multiply, often three to five times or more.

For example, if you're pulling in $450,000 a year in revenue, you should invest around $1,875 per month back into your business. This strategy will strike an ideal balance between re-investment and profit generation.

That said, I understand if you have fear and hesitation around investing—especially if you have a new business. If you're asking, "How will I know if I'm investing my money intelligently?" Don't worry, you're not alone. But here's the deal: Risk is always involved in attaining the most valuable outcomes in life. Risk is inevitable.

To put this in perspective, think about your current customers for a moment. They spend thousands of dollars to fix their cars in what most people consider to be a very opaque (or "blind") transaction, right? However, they don't think of it as risk, but rather as an investment in long-term value and opportunity. Their mindset is: "When I invest money to get my car fixed, I'll get a lot more use out of it in the future," *not* "It's too risky to invest in my car."

When it comes to maintaining their cars, your customers have an "investment mindset" rather than a "risk mindset." You need an investment mindset about your business too.

To that end, your long-term focus should be explosive business growth while streamlining your customer generation process. But if your priority is to save as much time and money as possible, it may suit you well to hire someone to help you on your journey. I'll talk about that more up ahead.

Either way, the only way you will fully succeed is by understanding this law of business fully:

*The more time and money you invest in your business, the higher your exponential returns will be.*

When it comes to online marketing, you can either invest time and money to figure it out yourself, or you can ask a professional marketer for help. Either way, having an *investment mindset* is a necessary power source for your "marketing vehicle."

### *Primary Power Source #3: Lifetime Value of Customers*

To shed some light on the importance of investing in your business marketing strategy, consider how much total money you can make from one customer (their lifetime value).

In my experience working with auto shops, that value is around $3,000-$5,000. In other words, if you give your customers a great experience the first time around, they will most likely return multiple times because they trust you. Trust is everything!

Let's say you spend $500 to $600 to acquire a single new customer. Do you think of it as accruing additional costs, or investing money to get more money in return? Imagine trading $1 to get $10. $10 for $100. $100 for $1,000. That's how great business investments work: like winning a lottery, the money you invest multiplies.

The good news is, the acquisition cost of new customers will be much cheaper than $500 if you follow the effective marketing strategies I've shared in this book. However, to reach new cost-efficiency levels in your business, it helps to understand how the "marketing vehicle" works (the purpose of this book).

## Every Step Matters

In any vehicle, there is a "hierarchy" of steps or systems which govern how the entire unit runs. Every step matters. It is the same with this book. Every step matters.

Even if you find yourself feeling confident because you have completed some of these steps already, I strongly suggest you don't skip any chapters because I have added many important insights you might not be aware of.

I share details which most of my clients neglected prior to working together, the sort of details that will optimize your efforts and ensure none of your precious time and money are wasted.

## Step-by-Step Overview

Manuals rarely teach you how to use the tools required to build a product or machine—at least, not in detail. However, manuals do help the reader understand how components of a machine come together and work as a unit. This book is the same. In this case, the "machine" is an online marketing system.

I have many tool and strategy recommendations to share, but to detail them would require a book ten times this size. Therefore, as you make your way through this book, I encourage you to research further, learn how to use the recommended tools, and leverage this book as a "big picture" reference manual to guide you in the art and science of online marketing.

I wrote this book to share all the information and resources available to help you leverage online technology to acquire and retain more customers. You can discover how to do anything for free with Google. As the cliché saying goes, "Google is your friend."

I've done my best to simplify technical terms and concepts, but if you run across anything you have more questions about, reach out to me via the email address at the end of this chapter or search for additional information on the web. If you go the latter route, always check multiple sources.

At this point you may be wondering, "If I can do all the research on my own, what is the point of this book?"

If you apply its principles. This book can and will free you from the time burden of trying to figure out where and how to begin online marketing. There are millions of resources out there, but they are all over the board and many are misleading and/or generic. This book is specifically built for the automotive industry. As I'm sure you've seen, if you work with a generic marketing company that doesn't know your industry there's a good chance that you'll end up losing money.

This book will also help you discover what it takes to market yourself online so you can decide if you want to invest the time, do it yourself or hire a professional to help.

My primary aim, in the end, is to save you the time of figuring out your immediate path to business growth so you can take action with the least amount of stress and confusion and achieve your goals.

Why is that important? Because you'll never see the finish line if you start the race with no clue how to get to it. You need a map and a strategy to win the race, and I have provided the winning formula in these pages.

If you have any questions, go ahead and reach out to me at:

**jonathan@socialleafmarketing.com.**

# Part 1: Power Systems

Ignite and Fuel Your Marketing Strategy Online

# Chapter 1: Vehicle Systems Overview

Where Many Shops Go Wrong and How Not to Be One of Them

---

*"Failure is simply the opportunity to begin again, this time more intelligently."*

*-Henry Ford*

---

## What's in it for you?

By the end of this chapter, you'll have extreme clarity as to where and why many auto shops fall short on marketing strategy. By learning from others' failures, you'll understand how to *intelligently* manage your own business needs and avoid time-consuming and expensive "trial and error" disasters.

*Imagine this...*

You wake up tomorrow morning and your calendar is filling up with customer bookings via your simple, automated marketing system. Your staff is busy all day, and they're even requesting additional help because business is booming.

As your revenue begins to climb, you hire a few extra staff members. The profit margin widens, and the best part of it all is you know your success is solid and sustainable because you're employing a *tried and tested approach* to fuel your marketing process. Sound good? I'll be sharing exactly how you can make that happen in the pages ahead.

For now, let's look at what happens to shops who are NOT leveraging online technology for marketing and reputation management.

## Get Behind Your Customer's Steering Wheel

*Understand a customer's worst nightmare...*

Meet the typical, modern day auto repair consumer. We will call him Ralph.

Ralph is happily driving down the freeway, holding a sandwich in one hand and steering with the other as music blares in the background—when suddenly his car engine begins to stall.

With his heart racing, he turns down the music, taps the brake, and listens closely for any strange sounds. The check engine light is blinking. He pulls over to the shoulder.

Ralph is the kind of guy who doesn't like taking risks, so instead of trying to drive the car home, he immediately pulls out his phone and texts his friends, makes some calls to his family, gets a ride lined up, and calls for a tow truck.

The tow truck company asks, "Hey Ralph, where do you want us to tow your car?" Decision time. Ralph has never needed auto body repair before, so he doesn't have an immediate answer. What happens next is crucial.

Since Ralph is like most consumers, he will most likely:

- Search Google or Yelp for local auto shops. Having heard plenty of horror stories about dishonest auto shops, he doesn't want to wind up being a victim of one.

- Read online reviews of each local shop. If a shop doesn't have reviews, he immediately skips over it to find a shop with customer reviews.
- Check auto shop websites to see how legitimate and professional they are and learn what types of services they offer.
- Talk with his friends, get shop suggestions, and maybe go back to Google again to check reputations.

If you haven't figured it out, the "modern curse" I've been alluding to is the curse of not having a solid online reputation and presence. The internet gives your customers the ability to *challenge you.* Investigate you. Even become skeptical before they ever talk to you!

You see, no matter how a new customer finds you, they will only trust you if you have a good reputation online.

Most consumers—especially in this automated age—want to be *led by the hand* from start to finish. They need assurance of your trustworthiness before they step into your auto shop.

Many shops are still under "the curse" and not doing everything they can to build a glowing and unique online reputation. The result is that potential customers don't *trust* them with their vehicles. Trust is everything!

Ralph's greatest nightmare is choosing an auto shop only to find out months later (when his car breaks down again) that he was ripped off. That's why consumers spend a lot of time investigating their potential choices; no one wants to get ripped off.

## "Presence"

Even if your business has some good reviews online, it's equally important to have a prominent—even dominant—presence online.

***Presence.*** *Presence means being there to "meet" your potential customers wherever they go online.*

If your customer researches you on Google and social media platforms, you need to be wherever they go. Your mission is to always "be there" for them. You must prove you are familiar with their whereabouts. The easiest way to do this is simply by being *present* wherever they are and starting a conversation with them.

A great way to meet potential customers where they are is via email. Building relationships and expanding your reputation beyond the public space to have a "one on one" conversation is friendly and will appeal to their social habits.

We will talk about specific ways to start a conversation in the chapters ahead.

## Bad vs. Great Marketing Strategies

### *Bad Marketing Strategies:*

1. Do not prioritize *reputation.*

2. Do not focus on being *present* where potential customers are online.

3. Do not focus on relationship-building with potential customers to build trust.

***Great Marketing Strategies:***

1. Focus on being present where potential customers are online (i.e. Google search).

2. Prioritize reputation.

3. Focus on relationship-building with potential customers to build trust.

## What's Next?

In the next chapter, we'll get started building your marketing strategy with online reviews. Reviews will power your "marketing vehicle" and help you become *present* in your customers' online lives.

You will learn:

1. Why online reviews are the most important "power" component of your online marketing system.

2. How to get effective reviews that will grab the attention of prospects.

3. Best practices of online marketing to grow your business.

# Chapter 2: Fuel Your Business' Reputation

## Reviews: The Single Most Effective Piece of Auto Shop Marketing

---

*"When a management with a reputation for brilliance tackles a business with a reputation for bad economics, it is the reputation of the business that remains intact."*

*-Warren Buffet*

---

The coolest cars have a story behind them (think Dukes of Hazzard). Your shop is no different. You must have riveting customer stories behind your business.

By the end of this chapter, you will know how to get powerful online reviews to immediately begin strengthening your reputation. I'll walk you through the simple process.

## Why Online Reviews are the First Step

If potential customers believe your business is untrustworthy, then your other marketing efforts won't matter. People will *not* give your business a chance unless they experience a positive *social signal* indicating your shop is reputable.

***Social Signal.*** *Using what your other customers say about you to quickly earn your status as a trustworthy business.*

What's in it for you? You can leverage positive things your customers say about you to quickly earn your status as a trustworthy business if you focus on acquiring powerful online reviews. With a proper marketing strategy, massive profits can and will follow. However, if you don't prioritize online reviews, your other business strategy efforts will be ineffective and/or costlier.

In other words, all your other efforts are dependent on your reputation. So, if you focus on your reputation first, your entire journey to profitability will be much easier.

Many automotive shops employ marketers who do a decent job, but they often overlook the importance and power of online reviews. Even with a brilliant marketing campaign, you'll be losing customers and money if you don't have good ratings on Yelp and Google.

You wouldn't believe how many shop owners tell me they don't pay attention to their online reviews. They may as well be saying, "I refuse to pay attention to my customers."

**Paying Attention.** *If you don't pay attention to your online reviews, you're not paying full attention to your customers.*

The most successful businesses monitor and analyze customer feedback and act on it quickly to improve *customer experience.* So for example, if a customer has a bad experience with the shop hours being inaccurate and shows up when the shop is closed, you should be notified immediately so you can take a direct action to address the problem.

*Here's the good news…*

Once you implement some riveting reviews into your marketing strategy, they will produce an inevitable "domino effect" on your business. Your advertising return on investment will be awesome, your customers will have a better experience, and ultimately, *you will make more money.*

On top of all that, your confidence and pride in your company will increase ten-fold. If you *know* your customers think your shop is the best shop in town, your morale and overall happiness level will soar. And customers will notice your happy demeanor and say even *more* good things about you!

Once you decide to get on board with prioritizing your reputation through online reviews, the question remains...

"Where do I get started with online reviews, and how do I ask my customers for them?"

## Pump Fuel Into Your Business with Riveting Reviews

By the end of this section, you will know:

1. The difference between a mediocre review and a riveting, profitable review (which will influence

potential customers to trust and invest in your services).

2. How to ask your customers for riveting reviews (so you can build a reputable foundation to pillar your other marketing efforts on).

3. How to "install reviews" into your marketing vehicle and accelerate your business.

***Mediocre Reviews Vs. Riveting Reviews***

Pop quiz time. Read the reviews below. Which reviews would you consider riveting and which would you consider mediocre?

- **Review 1:** "I highly recommend them."
- **Review 2:** "I have been to MANY other shops before. This one is the best."
- **Review 3:** "My car was having trouble and these guys fixed it up in no time. Great service."
- **Review 4:** "My check engine light came on last week, and I started to notice a weird grinding noise. When I called these guys, they let me know exactly

what the problem could possibly be. I brought my car in, and it was fixed in no time. Great service."

- **Review 5:** "I will definitely come back again!"
- **Review 6:** "These guys are honest and trustworthy. I will definitely come back again!"

If you said review numbers 2, 4, and 6 are riveting and 1, 3, and 5 are mediocre, congratulations! You're already getting the hang of it. The mediocre examples are less detailed and powerful than the riveting reviews. The riveting reviews also explain the positive features of the shop.

***Three Qualities of a Riveting Review***

Here's an easy way to recognize a riveting review. Riveting reviews generally have one to three great qualities called *comparison, crud, and character.*

1. **Comparison:** A riveting review shows/tells people how *your shop* is BETTER than others.
2. **Crud:** A riveting review details the nitty-gritty problem or pain your customer was having prior to working with you.

3. **Character:** A riveting review expresses how you and your staff are trustworthy and honest.

With those three C's in mind, go ahead and read the mediocre and riveting reviews again. Do you see the pattern of *Comparison, Crud, and Character* now?

***Three Things People Need***

Deep down, every potential client with a car problem needs three things:

1. **Validation.** They are fearful of being ripped off by a shop.

2. **Reassurance.** They are in pain (i.e. stressed out, freaked out, etc.) due to their car troubles.

3. **Trustworthy Solution**. They are looking for a trustworthy person and shop to help solve their problem(s).

Your reviews should reflect these needs so potential customers see your ability to *empathize* with them. Otherwise, your reviews will be mediocre and people will not seek your services.

In other words, human beings need to feel a sense of safety and assurance that your shop will solve their *specific* problem/pain. They want to surround themselves with reliable people. A *riveting review* assures them that you will meet all three needs.

## How to Get Riveting Reviews

In short: Ask for them. If you've been in business a while, you probably have some long-time customers, right? Fortunately, your satisfied customers will be open to helping you. You just have to know how to ask.

*I know what you're thinking…*

"But Jonathan, isn't it a bit shady to ask for reviews from my customers?"

No! You're simply helping them put how you have *genuinely helped them* into words. It would only be shady if you asked them to say something that wasn't true.

If you can learn how to ask for reviews, you'll have much more control over your online reputation. Better yet, as shop owners who've worked with me can attest, your revenue will increase. So please don't skip this step. Like I said in the introduction, your reviews are a *primary power source* for your Marketing Vehicle.

## Three Proven Steps to Get Riveting Reviews

1. **Choose** a review platform and configure it.
2. **Pick** a communication platform.
3. **Make** a specific review request to your customers.

### *Choose a Review Platform*

At SocialLeaf Automotive, we use Google as the primary review platform for our clients. Theoretically, you could use a social media channel for your primary review platform but we do *not* recommend it. Why? Because most people search via

Google, and it's very difficult for them to find your social media account via Google search.

**Review Platform.** *A place where your potential customers can go to see all your reviews and obtain proof you are trustworthy/credible.*

Additionally, Google is much easier to integrate with effective advertising strategies, has no barriers to access (such as membership requirements), and overall your chances of reaching a large audience are higher on it.

Creating a "Google My Business" page is the first step you must take to add your business review platform to Google.

### *Configure Your Review Platform (Google My Business)*

1. **Go** to https://www.google.com/business/.

2. **Click** on "Manage Now."

3. **Log in** to your Google account. If you don't have one, click on "Create Account."

4. **Enter** your business name. Make sure you include a relevant keyword that describes your business function here. For example, including the keyword "auto shop" would be a good idea.

5. **Choose** "Yes" to add your location to Google Maps.

6. **Enter** your business address on the next screen.

7. **Click** "Yes or No" to the question: "Do you serve customers outside of said location?"

8. **Add** the areas you serve (if yes to the previous question).

9. **Select** your business category.

10. **Enter** your contact information. Make sure you input your website address.

11. **Follow** the final instructions for your business verification.

Once your business has been created (Google will send you a verification postcard and it can take a week or more to receive), go back to the Google My Business home page and click "Get More Reviews" and copy the link. This is the link you will be sending to your customers to solicit a *riveting review.*

### ***Choose a Communication Channel***

This is the channel(s) you will use to solicit reviews from your customers. You can email, ask in person, or send a text. Most of our clients find text messages to be the most effective. All you need is three to five *riveting reviews* and you'll be off to an amazing start.

Pro Tip: Use a platform like BirdEye or Grade.us to send review requests via text.

### ***Make a Specific Review Request to Your Customers***

Think about your best, long-term customers right now. Three to five of them. These are the customers you should contact first. Why? Because they will be most willing to write *riveting reviews* for you. Again, as long as they are being honest, there is nothing wrong with asking them for help.

Here's an example email you can send to your best customers:

Subject: Looking for some help

Hey John,

Just reaching out to thank you for being a loyal customer at <Name of company> for so long. I'm wondering if you could help me out with something really important. Can you please leave a positive review on Google for our auto shop?

We would be grateful if you could refer to:

1. The problem we helped you with.
2. How you feel about our staff.
3. What makes us your first choice.

Here's the link to our online review page: http://www.linktopage.com.

Thanks in advance!

Notice, the communication is simple, honest, personable, and specific.

*The more specific you are, the more people will want to help you.*

Just make sure you do all of the following in your communication:

- Thank the customer for their business and loyalty.
- Be transparent and direct about your intention.
- Provide the link to your Google My Business page with details about what you'd like them to write. You could even send them a template or example. This works well if you want a longer and more detailed review. People are willing to help if you give them the exact steps they need.

*You're off to a great start…*

Focusing on high-quality reviews from the beginning is critical to your success. When your future happy customers see your *riveting reviews*, they will be inspired to add their own. Imagine having tons of *riveting reviews.* Tons of riveting reviews = higher profits!

## Pro Tips

### *Review Automation*

If you use shop management software, you can often set it to automatically email the customer a review request through whichever channel you specify. Also, shop software can deliver automated service reminders and "thank you" emails.

If you don't have shop software, strongly consider looking at different options. Check out Capterra.com to see software reviews and compare by features. See how important reviews are? You'll probably be using them to evaluate which shop software you decide to go with.

### *Damage Control*

Once your business continues to grow online, you'll have to manage your reviews. Some of your reviews may be negative—which can be costly (20 customers per negative review on average). However, if you respond promptly, you can often make amends and even get the customer to remove or change the negative review.

Here's an example of a simple response that works well for us with a negative review.

"Hi George, we're sorry to hear that your expectations weren't met, please contact us so we can get this sorted for you."

Alternatively, you can work with us at SocialLeaf Automotive to manage your reviews. We have developed a proprietary system to increase the number of online reviews you're getting. Additionally, we actively manage all reviews and always respond to negative reviews immediately.

As I mentioned, each ignored negative review can *cost* you as many as 20 new customers on average, so this area is vitally important to manage.

## What's Next?

You just learned how to ask customers for a review of your business. Congratulations, you've learned a powerful skill and added a primary power source to start igniting your profits! Ch-ching!

Of course, all of this begs the question: How will potential customers find you online to read your riveting reviews? Good news: That's exactly what we'll be covering in the next chapter.

# Chapter 3: Local SEO: Your Marketing Vehicle's Ignition

How to be Easily Found by Eager Local Customers

---

*"The purpose of a business is to create a customer"*

*-Peter Drucker*

---

Online reviews without Local SEO are like a tank of gas without an ignition.

By the end of this chapter you will understand the basics of local search engine optimization (SEO) and how to use SEO tools to help eager customers find you quickly and easily online.

## Local SEO Overview

SEO stands for "Search Engine Optimization." Local SEO gives you the opportunity to get your business listed on the front page of Google when people in your area search for local auto shops.

Just as the ignition system sends a signal from the battery to the sparkplugs to power the vehicle for travel, Local SEO allows you to transmit a signal from your business to your potential customers so they will travel to you and pay for your services.

Even a fully-assembled vehicle won't go anywhere until the ignition starts. The same holds true with Local SEO. That is, your entire business might be fully-assembled online, but if no one can find it, it won't go anywhere. That's why SEO is the next most important step you must take to build your online marketing system.

## Why Local SEO is Your Next Step

The internet is like a giant *dark ocean* with a ton of fish (businesses). The fish are swimming beneath the surface, but fishermen (potential customers) can't see them from above. However, if a fish jumps up through the surface, it's a different story.

In the same way, no one ever will *see* your business online unless you find a way to "jump through the surface of Google" and show up on the search results page.

No matter how great your business is, it's one of a trillion fish in the dark ocean of the internet. Nobody knows where you are in the ocean. You must construct a way to jump up through the water's surface and catch your customer's attention.

Local SEO helps your customers locate you in a vast ocean of businesses. Specifically, it allows them to find you when they search for auto shops in their area.

If you don't implement solid SEO, you'll be losing time, energy, and money on a marketing strategy that goes to waste—because no one will even see you. Even if you have customers willing to post high-quality reviews for you, there is a high probability no one will ever see those reviews without effective Local SEO.

## My Promise to You

If you learn about Local SEO and apply it to your business, you will establish an online "territory" and become an *authority* in your trade. People with car problems will be able to easily find you for help. Think about how Ralph pulled out his phone and searched Google for auto shops. If you want to meet customers where they are and be the shop they call for help, you need Local SEO.

If you apply all the principles in this chapter, your marketing efforts will ignite profits, and any other systems you put in place will be a thousand times more effective. How? They will be genuinely *powered* by authentic local customers.

That said, your business and local market is different than everyone else's, so systematic experimentation on your part will be required to find out exactly how to get these principles to work *optimally* for your business and area.

I will provide some fundamental tools and step-by-step instructions in this chapter, but if you want to fast-track your way through the Local SEO phase, reach out to me directly through email anytime here: jonathan@socialleafmarketing.com.

## How to Get Your Business on Google and *Ignite* Your Local Reputation.

In this section I will teach you:

1. How to automatically attract more customers to your website through Google search.

2. What to do next once you've accomplished step #1.

*Look at Ralph's situation again...*

When Ralph searched Google for "auto repair," the highest-ranking businesses (as well as any shops appearing in Google Maps) showed up first in his search results.

***Rank.*** *When your business ranks high in Google, it will appear at the top of your potential customer's search results.*

Many factors determine your search results ranking, so I will cover each one, from most important to least important

Most people who search for businesses in Google are in a hurry, so it's really important the first thing they see is *you*.

For the most part, most people have short attention spans and won't spend their time sifting through a ton of pages to find an auto shop. This is why it's really important to be one of the first businesses they see in their search results.

## Step-by-Step Process for Local SEO

1. **Create** a "Google My Business" Page (if you haven't already).
2. **Join** Online Directories.
3. **Build** Your Social Media Platforms.
4. **Add** Links to Begin Link-Building.

### *Create a "Google My Business" Page*

Feel free to skip this step if you already built a Google My Business Page in the previous chapter.

Google My Business is a free business profile page that allows you to present all your important business information to customers in one place—although the ultimate benefit is to improve your rank in search results.

Once you verify your business, you will be able to see your profile page dashboard. You can see this page without verification, but you cannot fully manage your business in Google without completing verification.

On the left side of the dashboard, you'll see different parts of your profile that can be managed, such as: Posts, Info, Insights, etc. Take your time to explore this space. Also, take note of these best practices:

1. Make sure you're posting accurate hours of operation (found under *Info).* The easiest way to get *negative* reviews is by posting inaccurate hours of operation.

2. Include photos of you, your shop, and staff (found under *Photos).* You will build trust by doing this. It is vital for your reputation.

3. List your services that you provide right on your GMB page.

4. Respond to Google My Business reviews.

5. Use posts to promote events, offers, and content.

6. Add a shortname.

7. Add a description and complete your profile until it hits 100%.

### *Get Your Business Listed in Online Directories*

Getting listed in online directories is like injecting your marketing system with a *fuel additive*. How so? The more places your business is listed online, the more Google trusts it as a legitimate business whose reputation is worthy of high search results ranking.

Online local business directories will usually list your business for free, so passing this opportunity up would be a bad idea.

### Find Local Online Business Directories

1. **Research** "online local business directories" on Google.

2. **Create** a preliminary list of potential candidates.

3. **Investigate** which directories are the most popular,

4. **Remove** undesirable candidates from the list.

**Join Directories**

1. **Create** an email address for your listings. Gmail will do. You may be a target for a fair amount of spam, so having a designated email account will prevent clutter and "inbox chaos."

2. **Pick** one directory to start with, then add one directory per day so you don't get overwhelmed.

3. **Verify** your business name, address, and phone number (NAP) are the same for all directories.

### *Get on Two Big Social Media Platforms*

Maybe you have social media pages already. If so, how are they doing? Have you been keeping them alive and active? Active social media pages send signals that you're engaged and Google will rank you higher in their search results.

Make sure your business name and location are consistent across these platforms as well. If you don't have social media pages yet, or you want to start over, here are some ideas for you:

1. **Get Facebook and Instagram**. These are the two main platforms we recommend for our clients. On Facebook, you'll need to create a Page for your business. Because Facebook and Instagram are constantly updating their interface, as with any social media platform, go to Google and search: "how to create a Facebook/Instagram business page in 2020" (or whatever year it is) for Facebook.

Here's another Google search trick that will save you tons of time. At the top of the Google search page, you'll see a horizontal menu (Images, Shopping, News, et al). Scroll to the right, select Search Tools, Any Time, then Past Month. Viola, no more old, irrelevant search results!

2. **Get Hootsuite.** Hootsuite is essentially a "giant control panel" where you can manage all your social media posts from one place. A major time-saver!

3. **Update Your Pages** at least once per week. Never let more than a month go by without an update.

This is a bare minimum. The more often you can update, the better.

## Pro Tips

Repost your social posts on your Google My Business Page. This will help Google understand that you're an engaged and active business owner—which is vitally important. We provide this service for all our Local SEO clients on a weekly basis. In the post description, include keywords that you want to rank higher, i.e. "BMW service." Google will pick up on these keywords and rank your business higher in its search results.

### *Begin Link-Building*

If you've ever been on the internet and seen underlined, clickable text (often blue or other colors), you've seen a *link*.

Link-building is the art of getting links to your website placed all over the web so Google will understand how trustworthy you are and raise your search results ranking.

Much like traditional SEO, links are a great way to get ranked higher for Local SEO. The more links pointing to your page, the higher your ranking will be.

How do you get links to your website placed all over the web? Reach out to other relevant local sites, people on social media, etc. (basically anyone who owns a website and is willing to add your link) and politely ask them to put your link on their website. Here are a few ideas to start with:

1. Chambers of Commerce
2. Local business groups
3. Local business directories

4. Local newspaper sites

5. Family and friends

6. Previous customers

If you want other ideas, you can easily research and discover what other business owners like you have done to succeed. Use a tool like Ahrefs or Moz Link Explorer to see where your competitors are getting links from so you can get those same links too.

Don't get me wrong. There's a lot of information out there, and it's tough to figure out what works and what doesn't. Therefore, you'll need to patiently test approaches and adjust as necessary. The important thing is that you get started right away. Link building is not easy, in fact most SEO firms that claim to be SEO experts don't know how to link build, and if you're not link building you're missing a vital piece of SEO.

And don't forget about riveting reviews! I cannot emphasize their importance enough. Reviews are a great way to build credibility. Genuine, positive, riveting reviews aren't hard to get. Just ask. Our clients use text messaging to boost reviews on the review platform of their choosing.

Don't forget, when you get riveting reviews (five stars!) you'll be building trust with customers before they even enter your shop. You'll also be building trust with Google. If Google sees your company is admired by many people, they will move you up the rankings ladder. The higher your business ranks, the more customers will be able to find you in the vast internet ocean!

As you learn more about SEO and your rankings improve, you will become one of the top-ranking auto shops on the search results page when people in your community search for auto repair.

## What's Next?

So far, we've addressed two power sources in your marketing system: Online reviews (fuel for your business), and Local SEO (ignition for your vehicle) Once you apply these power sources, Google will know your business and people will be able to find your listing *quickly and easily*.

Not only that, but with public admiration for your business via riveting reviews, you will have laid a foundation to leverage Local SEO to become known as a *local authority and trustworthy auto-shop* in your community and your profits will begin to increase.

In the next chapter, we will super-charge your online presence with Website SEO to further boost your rankings in the search results.

# Chapter 4: Rev Up Your Marketing Vehicle With Website SEO

Harness the Power of Google Search

---

*"Google's done a super good job on search; Apple's done a great job on the IPod."*

*-Bill Gates*

---

Google accounts for 85% of web traffic, so it's far and away the most important search engine.

## What's In It For You?

By the end of this chapter, you will have begun to optimize your website for success. In a way, you will have "introduced your website to Google" properly so Google and your site can communicate with one another as friends, rather than strangers who don't know each other.

Without Website SEO, your website is like a lone tumbleweed: aimless and detached from the rest of the outside world. None of your website content will matter if it is nothing more than a floating "blob" of data, never having been properly optimized for Google.

The goal with this step is to fully connect your site to the systems you put in place in the previous chapters so everything can work together smoothly, like a finely-tuned engine.

## Why Website SEO is Your Next Step

You've received some riveting reviews, you're beginning to establish "local domination" with your *Google My Business* profile, and perhaps you've even got your business listed in some directories. Nice work!

Now it's time to ensure potential customers have a resource to really get to know you. I'm talking about a place that displays your true colors, shows off your track record, and builds customer trust. That place is your website.

To understand the importance of your virtual business home, think about your auto shop. In your auto shop, you've probably have an area where customers make payments and receive their car diagnoses, right? That is, you don't make them stand in the garage amidst the grinding gears and kerplunk of tools. I'm sure your auto shop provides a space for customers to converse with you, describe problems, and transact.

Your website is also a place for the customer. It's the principle way you connect your website to Google and provide customers a space to form a bond with you and investigate your business on a deeper level.

Now you might be wondering: "OK, Jonathan, but will this directly boost my rank on Google?"

Yes! Per the analogy above, Website SEO is connected to Local SEO and will *boost* your local search rank. Website SEO drives traffic to your website at a low cost; therefore, we highly suggest taking a few important steps to ensure best results.

***Traffic****. This term has nothing to do with your nearest highway. Web traffic refers to the people who visit your website through various channels.*

This chapter covers the two types of Website SEO you must perform: On-Page Website SEO and Off-Page SEO and provides best practices for both. If the content presented here seems a little too technical—and thus abstract—after the first read, I encourage you to re-read as necessary. I sometimes read chapters—even whole books—multiple times to fully comprehend them.

## On-Page SEO

On-Page SEO refers to things that can be done on *your* website to improve its traffic and Google rankings. Just as human beings communicate with one another in common languages, your website and Google communicate with each other in common languages also.

As you may know, when it comes to websites, there is more to them than meets the eye. All websites are made up of lines of computer *code* that determine what is displayed and what actions can be performed by the visitor.

To help you understand this, imagine reading a news article about a recent natural disaster across the world. You read words on the page as a language, then your imagination gives you a picture and feeling of what took place during the event. In a sense, you "re-live" the event when you read about it.

In the same way, there are "words" of a computer language behind the scenes of a website, and what you see on the front page is the final image, text, etc. they portray.

**Source Code.** *The computer words behind the scenes are known as the website's source code (also known as website language). The behind-the-scenes source code can be edited by you (or a website programmer you hire) to change appearance and features of your website.*

As you can probably guess, website source code includes a ton of strange symbols. If you get a chance to look at it, you'll see different symbols, such as "< >" and many others.  It's a symbol-based language, and it takes some time to learn.

If you're inclined to dive into your website's source code, feel free to conduct some Google research to find the resources and tools to get started.

At any rate, your website source code is most likely not configured by default to "talk" to Google. This is where On-Page SEO comes in. On-Page SEO consists of changing your website source code so Google can read it, make sense of it, and *welcome* you into its search and rankings world. When all is said and done, your website will be Website SEO-optimized and more people find you.

To be clear, the visible, customer-facing text on your web pages also matters in SEO, but for now we're going to focus on the source code "under the hood."

### *On-Page SEO Best Practices*

Disclaimer: Configuring On-Page SEO requires training and ingenuity. Therefore, you might consider hiring someone to do it for you. Check Fiverr.com for inexpensive programmers (and only hire those with plenty of five star—riveting!—

reviews). On the other hand, if you have the time, you can learn to do it yourself.

If you go the DIY route, research and study will be required to learn how to navigate the backend of your website with a website development program. It's definitely doable; it's just a matter of time and effort.

Regardless of which way you go, it's important to understand the basics. Get familiar with the list of items below. If you're up for learning, search for additional help in Google. And of course, if you get frustrated, just hire a professional.

### *Title Tags*

Title tags tell Google what your website is all about. In the image below, the title is the largest text at the top. The only places you'll see title tags are in search results, the tabs on your browser, and in the source code of your website.

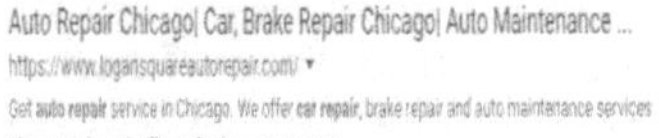
Auto Repair Chicago| Car, Brake Repair Chicago| Auto Maintenance ...
https://www.logansquareautorepair.com/
Get auto repair service in Chicago. We offer car repair, brake repair and auto maintenance services Chicago and near by Illinois. Book an appointment.

Title tags should be 55-60 characters in length. Your "home page" title tag should include a "main keyword" that explains what you do.

### *Keywords*

People use keywords to search Google. "How to fix my car" is a *keyword phrase.*

When you include keywords such as "fix" and "car" in your website tags, you help Google understand your website has relevant content to display to people searching for auto repair shops.

In other words, if your home page has the phrase "auto repair in Chicago," then when a user searches for a phrase with similar keywords, Google will show them your website (of course only if you have earned a high ranking by doing the other things I have described in previous and subsequent chapters).

### *Meta Description*

A meta description is a block of descriptive text that informs Google (and people searching it) what your website is about. It's a "teaser" that gives web surfers a glimpse of what's ahead.

I have placed a rectangle box around the meta description in the screenshot below.

Auto Repair Shop Chicago | Car Repair, Service & Maintenance ...
https://chicagomotors.net/ ▾
**Chicago** Motors is an **auto** repair **shop** in **Chicago** that provides expert car repair services. We specialize in BMW, Mercedes, Audi, Land Rover, Volkswagen, ...

It says, "Chicago Motors is an auto repair shop in Chicago that provides expert car repair services. We specialize in..."

Important note: The meta description in the example above contains the *location* of the auto shop and primary "occupation" keywords (auto repair shop). Yours should too.

Your meta description should:

- Be less than 155 characters.
- Include your main keyword and city location.
- Include powerful text that communicates your *authority*.

For example, a sound meta description might read: "Logan square auto repair, Chicago's #1 mechanic and auto repair shop." That's authoritative.

If you're unsure about what to include in your meta description tag, simply conduct some competitive research. See what top-ranking local auto shops have implemented. The same rule applies to all other steps.

### *Header Tags*

The easiest way to understand header tags is by example. Let's say you go to an auto shop website and the following text appears on the home page:

**#1 Auto Shop in the World**

Servicing in Chicago, IL.

These are examples of header tags in the source code being displayed on the website. Google likes them and uses them to connect searches with relevant results.

Some website builder platforms, such as WordPress, allow you to easily change tags in a user-friendly interface.

At any rate, make sure your page includes header tags with primary keywords that describe your work.

### *Keyword Phrases*

Keyword phrases describe concepts. For example, say you specialize in BMW repair. You may want to include the keyword phrase "BMW repair" on your home page a few times so when Google "crawls" the page, it understands what your business is all about and shows it to BMW owners. Keyword phrases essentially create a dialogue with Google (and other search engines).

Once *Google* knows you are a safe and legitimate "BMW repair" shop, they will help you win in your market by ranking your website higher. Consequently, many people will see your business and visit your website.

However, getting a high ranking on Google's front page is not as simple as choosing great keywords. Many shops like yours are competing to get to the top of search results. You will need a well-rounded SEO strategy that *leverages* all the components we are discussing here.

In that spirit, I recommend conducting *keyword research* to uncover the most profitable language for your web site.

Pro Tip: If you don't want to keyword research yourself or you don't have the tools(Ahrefs, Moz Pro), hire a freelancer from Fiverr.com to conduct keyword research.

### ***Keyword Research***

This is the process of discovering which words your prospects are most likely to use for *your* product or service when searching Google.

For example: In the state of Illinois, a million people a month may search for "Auto repair in Illinois." Another group of people may search for "Auto shops in Illinois." Conducting keyword research will reveal what people are searching for and how many are searching for it.

While your Google search engine rank does not depend exclusively on your keyword choice, it is a very important factor.

Keyword Research is a vast field and thus there's a whole lot of conflicting information out there. Here are some best practices that will serve you well.

**Well-Rounded Approach.** The secret to keyword research is to have a *well-rounded* approach. Use a variety of tools to discover potential ideas and make a final choice after examining all the options. If you're new, try and go after less competitive keywords. Understand that in your niche the words auto repair and car repair will have the most people *fighting* to rank for them.

**Tools.** The best free tool I've found for conducting Keyword Research is right inside Google Ads. It's called the "Keyword Research Tool."

**Education.** Get educated. Take the time to find what process works best for you. You have to find out which approach is most efficient given your learning style and so forth. There is no right or wrong when it comes to research. I recommend reading Matthew Capala's excellent book *Keyword Research Like a Pro.*

Regardless of your chosen approach, just make sure your efforts achieve these important keyword outcomes:

- Make sure your home page has location-specific keywords (i.e. "Auto repair in Chicago").
- Make sure the keywords for your other content pages, such as your blog, are related to a car repair problem people are seeking a solution for.
- Make sure your content benefits and serves people's needs. For example, do not talk about your products and services too in-depth. Keywords should be linked to helping people solve problems. The more problems you help them solve, the more they will trust you.

For example, a blog post titled "How to Change Your Oil" helps people solve a problem and establishes you as a trustworthy authority. The key is to speak to a pain point or trouble your potential customer may be having. Serve your website guest by helping them solve a problem!

### ***Internal & External Linking***

Be sure to link your web pages to each other. Additionally, link to other credible websites. This is another indicator of strong credibility to Google.

For example, let's say your mechanics are ASE-certified. It would help to have external links to ASE's website when your content mentions the credibility of your mechanics.

### ***Web Page URL's***

Each web page URL should have the topic of the page in it. For example, a page called "transmission flush" should be titled:

logansquareautorepair.com/*transmission-flush*

### ***Images***

Images are an easy way to tell Google even more about your website. When you upload an image, the filename should have the main keyword of the page in it.

For example, if your auto shop is in Logan Square, Illinois, you could have a home page image titled auto-repair-*logansquare.*

### *Alt-Text Images*

When you upload an image to your site, you can go into the source code and write what's called "alt-text." Alt-text displays if the image won't load, or if the user hovers their mouse over the image.

Why is alt-text important? Search engines use this data to figure out what your page is about. With multiple images, you can use a variety of approaches. For some images, the alt-text can be strictly keyword-focused, while other images can have alt-text describing what is going on in the photo, embellished with a few keywords.

### *Geolocation*

Geolocation is an advanced, but important, tool. Geo-tagging tells search engines *where your shop pictures were taken by using longitude and latitude data stored in the photos.* It's a quick and easy way to strengthen your local signal to Google and verify your credibility. If Google sees that your photos were taken in a certain location, they'll show your website to more customers in that location. Here's how to do it:

1. **Go** to: https://www.latlong.net/convert-address-to-lat-long.html.

2. **Get** the latitude and longitude readings of your address (copy and paste them into a Word Document).

3. **Go** to https://tool.geoimgr.com/.

4. **Click** on the "Drag Photos Here or Click to Upload" link.

5. **Upload** your image.

6. **Paste** your latitude and longitude readings below the map.

7. **Click** "Write EXIF Tags."

8. **Download** the Image.

9. **Add** the image to your Google My Business page.

***Page Speed***

The quicker your website loads, the more traffic Google will send to it. Have you ever been on a site that doesn't load within a few seconds? Pretty annoying, right? Here's how to speed up your website:

1. **Test** your Page speed. Go here:

https://developers.google.com/speed/pagespeed/insights/

2. **Enter** your web address into the field.

3. **Click** "Analyze."

Website speed runs on a scale of 1-100, so shoot for about 80. Once you identify the reason(s) your page is running slower than desired (which is revealed in the Google test), research various troubleshooting methods until you find one that fits your particular situation. A lot of WordPress site owners use a "caching" plugin for this very purpose.

### *Reduce File Sizes*

Reducing media file size is one of the quickest ways to enhance page loading efficiency. Google "how to optimize images for the web."

### *Website Hosting*

Chose a high-quality hosting company like *Siteground* to increase your page speed (siteground.com).

There are other possible options, so don't hesitate to conduct further research.

### *SSL*

SSL stands for "secure socket layer." Without an "SSL Certificate," Google will deem your page unsafe. Check to see if your website has an SSL certificate by looking at its URL. If it begins with "https," the site is secure. If it begins with "http" (no "s"), is not secure.

All you really need to know about SSL is that Google likes it, and it's a sign of a secure and safe site. To learn more about SSL and how to install it on your website, contact your web hosting support team or your dear old friend, me, you already have my email.

### *Blog Posts*

Having a blog is a powerful way to drive traffic to your website. As I mentioned before, the main keywords in your blog entries should relate to problems your potential customers are inquiring about. As Google search technology evolves, it's becoming critical to creating engaging and original content with tons of media (pictures, video, etc.) to improve ranking. Google loves originality.

If you're unsure what to write about, you can outsource your blog topic research. Go to fiverr.com to hire SEO specialists who can provide blog keywords and topics that will be the most profitable in your industry. Just make sure they are legitimate and have riveting reviews.

## Off-Page SEO

Off-Page SEO refers to source code adjustments that can be done on *other people's websites* to improve your website rank.

Off-Page SEO refers to actions taken outside of your own website that impact your rankings for search engine results pages (SERP's). This is accomplished when other reputable internet pages and sites promote and point to your website, effectively vouching for the quality of your content. It is a very similar concept to Local SEO, where citations point to your Google My Business Page and vouch for its trustworthiness. Of note it also has a considerable influence on your Local SEO.

How does Off-Page SEO help boost your Google rank? Simple: When another website publishes a link to your website, Google sees it and adds a bit of *trust* to your website profile behind the scenes. The link can either move the needle a little or a lot depending on the quality of the website. A quality link would come from a *very popular site* like the BBC or PBS. But all links from legitimate websites will help boost traffic to your website.

You can build links to your website through several different methods. You can pay someone to build them for you (hire an SEO agency), or you can ask another website owner to link to your website. In the latter case, the strategy is to create great content and share it around the web with a link to your website.

At any rate, all of these strategies are time-consuming, so I suggest taking care of the other marketing pieces before building links—or hire an SEO agency to do it for you.

In summary, the best thing about Website SEO is that it boosts your Local SEO efforts. The more Google trusts your website, the higher you'll rank for Local SEO search terms.

If you find yourself overwhelmed by any of this information, go back to the beginning of the chapter and read it again, making sure to understand each concept before moving to the next. Just focus on one step at a time and remember, Google is your friend.

## What's Next?

Now that you've got your marketing system foundation laid down (i.e. optimized Local and Website SEO, reviews in place to build credibility, etc.), you need to *start a conversation* with your potential customers when they reach your site. I'm talking about beginning a dialogue with them right when they walk through the virtual door to your website. The quickest way to do that is through *email marketing.*

# Chapter 5: Put the Rubber to the Road with Email Marketing

Be the First Shop on Your Customer's Mind

*"Efficiency is doing things right, effectiveness is doing the right things"*

*-Peter Drucker*

Listen to your customers, respond to them personally.

## What's In It For You?

By the end of this chapter, you'll know how to leverage email marketing to be the first repair shop on your customer's mind whenever they need service.

If you want to be the first shop to come to your customer's mind for auto repair, email marketing is an absolute necessity. Why? Because it's the *easiest* way to build a relationship with your customers from a distance and the simplest way to make sure your customers *remember* you amidst their stressful lives.

***Email Marketing.*** *Using email as a way to build a relationship with your customers so they remember* *you, prioritize you, and choose you to solve their car problems.*

If you have a first-time customer who goes a year without a repair, there is a chance they may forget about you or entertain other shop options the next time they have a problem. Effective email marketing will prevent that from happening.

Email marketing is conducive to relationship-building, *builds trust with your customer*, and establishes you as the "the one reliable shop" they can depend on.

If for whatever reason, you give your customers an ambiguous first impression, they may be open to exploring other shop options next time they have a car issue.

For example, if one of your first-time customers encounters another car problem down the road, they may hop on Google and search for "car repair." If your competitors have effective online marketing, they may win your customer over. Not good!

However, if you spend time consistently reaching out to your customers via email, *you will stand out.* They will believe in your credibility because you express genuine care and interest in them. Customers trust businesses that *consistently acknowledge their existence.*

## Why Email Marketing is Your Next Step

If you welcome someone into your shop through your website, you must acknowledge their existence and start a conversation with them.

*Think about it this way…*

It would be awkward to invite someone to dinner but completely ignore them when they showed up at your doorstep. That's exactly why email marketing is critical: it's a form of hospitality. It welcomes your customers into your world.

# How To Do Email Marketing, Build Relationships with your Customers, and Win More Business

In this chapter you will learn how to use email marketing to build relationships with your customers and win more business. Specifically, you will learn:

1. Good vs. Bad Email Marketing
2. Best Email Marketing Content
3. Email Marketing Setup
4. Email Marketing Best Practices

## *Good Email Marketing vs. Bad Email Marketing*

What do you do when you receive spam mail? You throw it away. Bad email marketing works the same way. If you send your customers boring emails *exclusively* with your service price tags, they will throw them away.

You might have *some* success because your name is showing up in their inbox, but if you want to *maximize* this platform, you must give your customer:

1. **Entertainment.** Make them laugh.
2. **Education.** Teach them something.
3. **Emotion.** Engage, impress, and inspire them.

If you pique your customers' curiosity with stories, helpful information, and/or humorous content, they will *want* to buy from you.

***The Money Effect.*** *Your customers pay money to whoever makes them feel good, brightens their day, and/or helps them solve a problem.*

### *The Best Email Marketing Content*

You might be wondering: "What should I send to my customers?"

I've worked with some shops who send out specials once a month, as well as some who periodically send out *educational content,* which is read more closely.

We've found great success by emailing educational content to our customers, which is fun to consume and *includes special offers* to entice them into the shop for a quick tune-up.

Any form of media (Blog Article, Email, Video, Podcast, etc.) which teaches your audience how to do something and/or solve a problem will generate interest.

Remember, the key is to help your customers solve a problem or brighten their day to make them feel good. For example, you could write an article titled, "How to find the correct tire pressure for my car?" and provide a link to the article in an email.

As your customers read that kind of information, they will *sense* your authentic intention and desire to help them. The better they feel about you, the more they will be inclined to pay you for your services.

Ultimately, the goal is to deliver *friendliness* and show your customers the skills and experience you have to solve their problems.

## Email Marketing Setup

Here is what I recommend for best results:

1. **Buy** a Web Domain (for your email marketing campaign).

2. **Get** MailChimp (to manage your email campaign).

3. **Build** Your Customer List.

4. **Send** Your Emails.

***Get a Web Domain Specifically for Email Marketing***

*Why?* If you send marketing emails out from your main domain, your *sender score* may be lowered—and if that happens, your domain reputation or sender score may be negatively affected and your ranking could suffer.

You might wonder why a low sender score matters. A low sender score means a higher probability of your emails being labeled "spam" and thus never seen by recipients. By purchasing a domain designated for sending emails, you won't have to worry about a low sender score.

Follow these steps:

1. **Go** to Godaddy.com.

2. **Search** for a domain name.

3. Once you find one that isn't taken, **buy** it. (You can usually find one between $5 and $20).

### ***Get Mailchimp***

Why? You need a platform to create and send your emails. With MailChimp it's easy to do this *automatically*, and track responses, etc. It is free up until you've acquired 2,000 contacts.

### ***Build Your Customer Mailing List***

Why? You need customer email addresses to send them emails. We've found the easiest way to do this is to ask for emails on customer paperwork. We've found that in general about 50% of customers provide their email address.

Something to note: Be sure to include a note next to the email field on your paperwork stating, "Don't worry, we won't spam you." If you assure your customers you aren't out to flood them with worthless information, they will be more inclined to share their email address.

Once you have a list of email addresses, put them into an Excel or Google Spreadsheet, then upload to MailChimp. Here's the process using Google Spreadsheets:

1. **Log into** your Google Account. If you don't have one, create one.

2. **Go** to Google.com, then search "Google Sheets."

3. **Click** on the top link, then click "Go to Google Sheets."

4. **Click** on "Blank" under the *Start a New Spreadsheet* section at the top.

5. **Create** your Column Names.

a. First Column: Email Address

b. Second Column: First Name

c. Third Column: Last Name

6. **Enter** data (name, email, etc.) into the appropriate columns.

***Send Your Emails***

Before proceeding, get to know MailChimp's interface. Explore the support section, dashboard, etc. When you're ready to send an email, do the following:

1. **Access** the area in MailChimp to import your emails.

2. **Open** your contact spreadsheet in Google Sheets.

3. **Import** the spreadsheet into MailChimp.

4. **Create** a new Campaign.

5. **Follow** the prompts and create your email (find an email copywriter on Fiverr.com if you need help formatting your email).

6. **Send** your email!

Keep in mind you can create multiple campaigns and configure them to send emails at certain intervals. Get to know MailChimp, it is a powerful tool for email marketing.

Pro tip: Authenticate your domain and dkim in MailChimp to improve your deliverability.

## Email Marketing Best Practices

Follow these best practices and you'll be guaranteed success.

### *Email Personalization and Segmentation*

The more targeted and personable your email, the higher the engagement rate. With MailChimp, you can segregate email lists in accordance with various characteristics, which is a great way to make your customers feel *heard and understood.*

For example, one list of emails may be customers who own vehicles with over 100,000 miles on them. Another list may be specific to customers who own a specific brand.

### *How to Avoid Being Labeled "Spam"*

There is an extensive list of technicalities involved in avoiding the spam box, but you should be okay as long as your emails are not robotic—write like a warm-blooded human—and don't go overboard with text. Also, don't send attachments or use tons of font colors, etc. Make sure your subject lines refrain from making exaggerated claims or include grandiose trigger words. For example, a subject line like this is a bad idea:

"Subject: FREE AUTO SHOP SERVICE!!!"

It makes for an unrealistic claim, is written in all caps, and just feels contrived. Be human and straightforward. Imagine you're reporting some important news to a friend. How would you write to them?

To ensure you have a thorough understanding of technical email regulations, check out the book *Email Marketing Rules* by Chad White on Amazon.com. It lists the most critical email marketing best practices.

### *How to Write Emails Well*

First off, subscribe to other newsletters online and analyze their writing style. Study and observe what's already on the market. Rewrite material that has already been written (in your own words, of course). You'd be surprised how much your writing will improve by rewriting others' material in your own style.

Most of all, pretend you are in a conversation with your audience. Use personable and simple conversational language just like the language I use in this book.

**Here's an example of a bad email:**

Subject: Get your PX-2500 at an INSANE price

To whom it may concern,

We have just released a new product and believe it will fulfill your needs sufficiently....

**Here's an example of a good email:**

Subject: Hey, Jack, have you hear about this?

Hey there,

You might have heard some weird grinding noises while driving. We were working on a car with that same problem and it almost went straight to the car graveyard. Good thing we managed to save it!

To celebrate, we've got a sweet deal to keep your car on the road. You can get your next oil change for 30% off….

See the difference? Be personable. Imagine you're speaking face to face with someone.

Writing well is an art that requires more knowledge than just the marketing how-tos. that I've shared in this book. I recommend researching "email marketing case studies" and reading books on how to communicate with customers through email. There's so much material out there you can learn—and much of it is cheap or free!

### *Link to Your Website*

Once you begin an email conversation with your customers, refer them back to your website periodically so they can get to know *you* while you help them. This is a great way to show them everything you offer rather than stuffing it all into a single email.

## Pro Tip

Use auto shop software to automate customer touchpoints that you don't have time for. For example, if a customer gets an oil change, send them an annual email reminder for the next oil change. Shop software usually pays for itself.

## What's Next?

In the next chapter, you will learn techniques to transform your website and compel your list of email subscribers to stop by the shop. It will be easy since you've already made a lot of progress with Local and Website SEO.

# Chapter 6: Clean Up Your Garage (Website)

Convert Browsing Customers to Paying Customers

---

"More business is lost every year
through neglect than through any
other cause."

-Rose Kennedy

---

Make 'em Feel at Home on Your Website.

## What's In It For You?

By the end of this chapter, you will know all the website best practices needed to convert curious prospective customers into *paying customers.* There is a basic structure for a website that we have found works best, and it is provided in this chapter.

Important note: Even if you already have a website, it's important to not skip over this section.

## Why Your Website is the Next Step

After you start a conversation with your customer via email, you need an easy and effective way to continue the conversation *automatically*. That's where website optimization steps in.

With a highly-organized and informative website, your customers can get to know you without making any phone calls. You won't have to spend as much time on the phone explaining your services to people, and you'll have more time to manage your shop and give customers the best results possible.

By optimizing your website, you'll also be centralizing all of your information, which will save you loads of precious time and energy. In other words, your website will act as a *spokesperson* for you, and you'll be able to focus on your specialty while the marketing takes care of itself.

*Your Customer's Journey...*

Though each customer takes a unique journey to your shop's doorstep, every journey needs to lead to *one familiar place* (your website) where they can find everything they're looking for.

If you don't build and structure this familiar place correctly, the customer may lose interest, get distracted, or—if your website lacks clarity and organization—even go into "information shock" and never make an order.

***Information Shock.*** *When your customer gets information from you in multiple places, but there's no single, central "home" for the information.*

Scattered and disorganized information makes it difficult for people to get a clear picture of who you are and what you can do for them. The remedy is to construct your website content in a way that puts your important information into one, easily accessible place.

## Website Optimization Basics

Here are some best practices you should adopt on your website.

### *Make it Mobile-Friendly*

In 2019, most of the traffic to your page will be mobile phone users (approximately 80%). If your website is not optimized for mobile, the layout can look scrambled, confusing, and incoherent. Consequently, visitors to your site will exit (or "bounce," which is a technical term for when people abandon a website without spending much time on it) and eventually go with your competitor.

It's important to remember that first impressions are everything. Make first impressions work in your favor to win more business. One of the easiest ways to do this is to get your website optimized for mobile users.

### *Hire a Professional Programmer*

Your website can be easily optimized for mobile users depending on the interface used to build it. You can hire a developer to figure it or, if you are very enterprising and have the time, you can research and do it yourself.

### *Use a Responsive Theme*

The most effective and pain-free way to build a website from the ground up is with a *responsive theme.*

**Responsive Theme.** *With this kind of theme, the website framework and source code have mobile optimization built-in already.*

As always, it's important to conduct plenty of research. Figure out how to optimize a page for mobile with your website's builder. Usually, there's an option in the website editor to move elements around and make them fit in a phone-sized screen.

**Test your website's mobile-friendliness:**

1. **Go** to this web page:

https://search.google.com/test/mobile-friendly.

2. **Enter** your website's address.

3. **Test** it out.

4. **Go** to your website on your smartphone to see what it will look like. This is a great extra check.

Theoretically, you could figure out how to edit your website's source code and optimize it for mobile, but it requires a lot of work on some platforms like Wordpress and is not recommended. In this case, hire someone to do it.

Note: It might be necessary to rebuild your entire site to make it mobile-friendly, depending on its underlying source code.

***Optimize Navigation***

If your website is not easy to navigate and all the information is densely packed like sardines, your customers will get confused and probably leave. While it's great to have a sleek-looking website with pleasing aesthetics, *function takes precedence over form.*

Customers just want to be able to visit your site quickly, view the information they need, and book or setup their appointment as soon as possible.

### Test Your Website Navigation

To test the user-friendliness of your website's navigation, ask yourself these questions:

Can people quickly find essential information, like customer reviews, hours, and special offers?

Is the information spacious or is it dense? In other words, is there enough *white space* between the big ideas so visitors can easily organize the information in their head?

For example, in this book you are reading there is white space between the big chapter headers so you know when a new idea is beginning. Approach your web content presentation in the same way. Visitors are hungry for visual ease and simplicity.

## Recommended Website Structure

Here are the *essential* pages you should have on your website:

### *Home Page*

This is by far the *most important part* of your website. There are certain components most new customers expect to see immediately or else they won't trust you. Here are the main components you should have on your home page:

**Reviews.** 90% of new customers want to know what other customers have said about you. Human beings have an innate need for proof of someone's trustworthiness through their "social status." The more riveting reviews you have, the higher your perceived social status will be to customers. Showcase your reviews on the home page to instantly build trust and bring in more bookings.

**Team Photos.** Be sure to have photos of you and your staff on the home page. You want to show other humans that you are just like them. Photos show you aren't hiding behind the online infrastructure of your business but rather offering a helping hand as a real person. Photos build trust.

**Hours and Location.** This information should be *highly visible* and located on the home page and contact page.

**Special Offers.** Keep it simple and powerful. Ask yourself: What one common problem can I solve that many customers need help with? Offer to solve it for a discount. Yes, it will temporarily cost you a bit to offer a discount, but the long-term returns are gigantic. Your customers will return if they have a great first experience. We will talk more about offers in a later chapter.

### *About Page*

An About Page is the second most visited page on a shop's website. Feature photos of yourself and the staff. Use bullet points to make important information easy to find. Most shop owners include a couple of fun facts about themselves, such as hobbies or what makes them unique. The idea is to make yourself seem personable, this helps build trust.

### *Services Page*

Most shop owners I work with have quite a few services available. To avoid information shock, a dropdown menu with each service works well. This way, the customer can easily find what they're looking for.

Service descriptions should be unique and original. For instance, if you are writing a description for a brake line flush, don't copy someone else's description. Put your own creative spin on it and write your own copy for each service. Google actually loves original content and will reward you for writing your own copy by giving your rankings a small boost.

Be personable with your writing voice to build trust and explain the benefits of the procedure. Focus on the benefits and highlight what the customer will gain from each service. You'll end up winning more sales.

Note: Benefits are *not* the same as Features. For example, if you're selling a "winter car tire," *snow friendly treads* are the feature. The benefit *is safety and easier winter driving.* Make sure you highlight how each feature helps the driver do the following:

- Saves the driver time, money, and energy.
- Helps keep the driver safe.
- Helps the driver enjoy the driving experience.

### *Blog*

This page is optional but helpful for SEO. As customers see more articles about unique car problems on your website, you will become an established authority in the auto care industry.

It's important to understand there are a lot of local car owners who look for free information about car problems. For example, for those looking to figure out the "whining noise" with their diesel vehicle, you could write an article about the topic, rank locally with good keywords, and win more customers by leading them to your website article.

The ultimate purpose of a blog is to inform, educate, and entertain your audience to build trust. It's also a great way to share your knowledge without overwhelming your readers. Make sure you keep the language simple. If you must get technical in your writing, always define terms for your readers. They will get bored with mumbo-jumbo. Always write as if you are conversing with a novice.

### *Testimonials*

Highlight riveting reviews and customer testimonials on this page. Include the person's name if possible (you'll need their permission), along with a star rating for each testimonial.

### *Contact*

Include details about your business name, address, phone number (in that order), email address, etc. Also, include a Google Maps plugin to show your visitors where your shop is located (a map will be displayed on the page). Also, include a simple contact form so they can email you from your website.

### *Online Appointment Scheduling*

Give your customers a way to set an appointment within the website if possible. There are tons of options out there, so research to find what works best for your situation.

### *Trust Icons*

Secure websites have "trust icons" to build trust with their visitors. Google "Norton Secured Seal" for installation instructions. You'll have to submit your website for verification.

## What's Next?

With all these steps in place, your customers will have a high sense of *security and safety.* If you have applied everything up to this point, you have everything you need to power your online marketing vehicle.

Now you need a way to "maintain" said power and attract the *exact* kind of customers you are looking for—customers who are *ready to pay* immediately. Without maintaining marketing power sources in your business, you may accrue a lot of interested prospects in the long run, but many will never buy from you. Moreover, you won't be able to track or predict how well your business is doing online.

You need a way to take an interested prospect from exclusively "interested" to "ready to buy." In other words, there are certain steps you must take to find people who are *immediately* ready to invest in your services.

The point of all the steps in this first section has been to bring your business to life online, giving it power and energy.

The next section is about making the most of your business life online and pulling in a *profit.*

# Part 2: Power Maintenance Systems

Prevent Burnout

and Excessive Costs.

Specialize in Your Market.

# Chapter 7: Stay in Your Lane With Offers

Get Customers to Take Action With Powerful Offers

*"If you don't have a good offer for your advertising, you're just branding "*

*-Unknown*

The difference between winners and losers is not power and speed, but direction.

The most powerful engine in the world is useless if it can't move the vehicle. If a vehicle cannot be steered or directed because the wheels are missing, the car is void of its practical value. There is no purpose for a vehicle that cannot travel, even if all of its internal systems are built out and connected.

Your business works the same way.

You can have powerful high-tech systems in place to get your website, reviews, and GMB page in front of your customers; however, if you don't lead them in *one powerful direction* with a narrow and specialized service offer, then your "vehicle" won't travel to profit.

In that case, you'll be revving your engine, showing off your talent, and aimlessly promoting your brand without gaining any income traction.

In the same way, you can have the greatest auto shop on earth, but if your new customer offers aren't compelling, you'll lose business to a competitor who understands consumer psychology better than you.

## What's In It For You?

By the end of this chapter, you'll know how to craft an irresistible offer so your customers know exactly what to expect and why it is valuable to them. Using the techniques I've shared, you'll be able to give them a sense of urgency, so they believe it's critical—perhaps even *necessary*—that they invest in your services (and no one else's) as soon as possible.

Of course, I can't make any numerical promises about your results, but the tips provided in this chapter will optimize your opportunities from the beginning.

## Why Offers are Your Next Step

With your power systems in place, you've created a way to attract new customers to your business online. However, when car owners get to your website, they need to know exactly how you can help them. They need assurance and proof you understand their *specific pain.*

Car owners want to know they aren't merely tossing their money into an auto shop, but rather investing money to solve a specific problem.

If you skip this step, your business may give the impression of being "some random shop that fixes cars," rather than "the shop that *specializes* in *fixing unique car problems.*"

People want and need specialization. In other words, they want specificity and understanding of their *unique* situation. That's where offers come into play (along with funnels—which I'll touch on in the next chapter). In this chapter I will cover:

1. Offer Basics
2. Anatomy of a Good Offer
3. Where to Place Offers

## Compelling Offer Basics

*Imagine for a moment...*

You're taking a summer road trip across the entire country. You've got a map and tons of junk food and energy drinks in the back seat to keep you awake. But your tank is running near empty.

Pretty soon, you'll have a problem. Without gas in the tank, you can't complete your road trip, which means all the effort of driving, planning, and getting excited to reach your destination could go to waste.

You could potentially lose the entire opportunity because you neglected a critical component of the trip: a full tank of gas. In other words, a full tank of gas is a valuable component of your overall success.

However, if you took a plane instead of a car, would a tank of gas be valuable anymore? No. Why? Because if you took a plane, your *situation* would no longer call for a car and gasoline. Therefore, we can say the value of the product (gasoline) is dependent on the situation and circumstance you are in.

In the same way, your product and/or service must speak to your customer's personal "pain point" and "time-sensitive" situation, solve an immediate problem, and fulfill a desire for the future. That is what a compelling offer does: it *heals* and *solves* specific pain points and obstacles for customers.

**Compelling Offer**. *An offer that: empathizes with your customer's current specific painful situation, solves their immediate practical problem and fulfills a time-sensitive desire for the future.*

For example, an "Oil Change" is not a offer. However, an "Oil Change With a 20% Summer Discount for a *Limited Time*" is a good offer. Why?

- The "summer discount" makes the offer season-specific. Seasons are powerful triggers that remind the customer of life needs. Seasons tied to discounts also remind the customer of how immediate and urgent an opportunity is.

- The discount percentage (20%) is specific. Specific discount numbers make the customer aware of how real, immediate, and urgent the chance to save money is.

- The "limited time" part amplifies the urgency of the situation. It helps the customer immediately understand how important their oil change is and what is at stake if they don't address it.

As they reflect on what is at stake, they think about what they desire in the future: to save money and make sure their oil is taken care of so their car will last for many road trips ahead.

In summary, a compelling offer is an *opportunity* that *influences* your customer to:

- Reflect on their current painful situation.

- Assess the urgency and importance of the situation.

- Consider what is at stake and how it affects what they desire in the future.

If you're wondering how to construct a compelling offer, fear not. That's what you'll be learning next.

## Anatomy of a Good Offer

It's important to understand the psychology behind offers so you can innovate and create them for your business. The more novel and creative the offer, the more customers will keep coming back. Here's an example of a simple offer on a website.

**DUE FOR AN OIL CHANGE?**

Or need one soon?

**Get 20% off an Oil Change TODAY**

Hurry! This Offer Expires on **August 28, 2020**

Click here to Claim Your Coupon:

**GET MY COUPON NOW**

---

Let's break this offer down piece by piece to understand why it works so well.

### *Clear and Specific Headline*

The headline "Due for an Oil Change" may not be perfect, but it addresses a specific time-sensitive problem.

### *Clear and Specific Body Text*

It uses numbers, dates, or percentages to convey specifics of the offer. "It takes just 5 seconds to click…" is a creative way to use specific numbers to convey how immediately tangible the opportunity is.

### *Discount*

Cost is one of the biggest motivators in a purchase, so offering a premium service for a discount can help make the offer irresistible.

### *Limited Time*

By limiting the time an offer is available you provide an environment of scarcity and thus urgency. Think of each offer as being a seasonal opportunity for you to gain new long-term customers. If you don't limit the time of your offer your potential customer subconsciously thinks "I'll get that done another day".

### *Call to Action*

A call to action (CTA) tells the user to take some specified action. In the example above, "Get My Coupon Now" is the call to action.

A call to action can be written as a command or action phrase, such as "Sign Up" or "Buy Now," depending on the context, and generally takes the form of a button or hyperlink. Make sure your call to action states the benefit the customer will get from completing the transaction

### *Additional Components*

Here are some other valuable ways to make an offer compelling:

**Limit Quantity.** If there's a way to limit quantity, the offer will help the customer understand how urgent their situation is. For example, "If you're one of the first 50 people to call and schedule an oil change, we will give you another 5% off!"

In this case, you would be limiting part of the offer to just 50 people.

**Risk Reversal.** As a consumer, there's a risk in every purchase. Every time a customer makes a purchase, they have decided the reward is greater than the risk and that they will benefit from making a purchase.

As an auto shop, there are things you can do to lower the risk for your customers. One of the best ways to lower the risk is by offering a warranty on the service.

Even a three-month warranty is invaluable and will help increase customer trust in your shop.

## Where to Place Offers

In the digital world, I recommend placing offers in the following places:

### *Website Home Page*

Your customers will visit your home page and immediately be drawn to your offer.

### *Website Landing Pages*

Landing pages are places in your website where customers "land" after searching for a specific need. Landing pages generally have one specific offer. More about landing pages in the next chapter.

### *Emails*

When your customers open their emails, they might be surprised to find you put your offer out at just the right time for them! As stated earlier, you can even time your MailChimp emails with seasons and other points in time.

### *Digital Advertisements*

In a later chapter, you will learn how to place your offers in front of ready to take action consumers.

## What's Next?

With your knowledge of offers, you have learned how to lead your customers in one specific direction, address a problem they are experiencing, and take them on a journey to trust your business for their auto repair needs

By understanding the basic anatomy and psychology of offers, you will be able to create a wealth of opportunities for your customers, so they feel there is *no other choice* but to return to you.

In the next chapter, you will learn how to position your offers to move your customers toward a purchase.

# Chapter 8: Carve Out a Parking Space with a Targeted Landing Page

Keep Your Customers Eyes on the Prize

*"The internet is a big distraction"*

*-Ray Bradbury*

In the online auto repair world, there is an excessive number of vague and generalized offerings, but not enough specific remedies for customer pain points.

*Too many auto shops are doing this...*

Offering too many options and not offering a true remedy for their prospect's pain.

Like I said in the last chapter, you've got to lead your prospects by the hand to your doorstep with simplicity. If you don't lead them, they will not follow you.

They are busy, overwhelmed, and stressed with all the options and opportunities they are inundated with from day to day.

They have seen hundreds and thousands of overwhelming offers that are too general and have too many options. They just want their specific problem solved right now.

There are way too many disorganized, vague, and boring websites out there, let's be a little different than everyone else.

Why not be the one person who truly cares about them, takes the burden off their shoulders, and makes their journey easy? If you're willing to go the extra mile for them, they will go the extra mile to buy from you!

In this chapter, you will learn how to make your customer's journey focused and direct with the creation and implementation of *landing pages.*

## What's In It For You?

Once you adopt the mindset and principles in this chapter, you'll be able to shut the door behind your potential customers once they enter your world.

They'll keep looking forward. They won't aimlessly wander around your website looking for the next corner to turn. Instead, they will feel an instinctive certainty about what next steps to take. That's the power of landing pages and funnels.

## Why Landing Pages Are Your Next Step

Remember the doctor analogy? For your customers to *trust and invest* in you, you need to solve their specific pain point immediately, or else the traffic you drive to your website will not be converted to paying customers.

Maybe some visitors will take the bait, but you will miss out on many opportunities without this step. By implementing landing pages, you will help customers see the next step clearly. In return, they will step right into your front door!

To help you visualize the importance of a landing page, think of it as a grocery aisle shelf with a specific food you are seeking. Notice how the store positions the product so you can easily find it and be on your way? That's the beauty of a landing page.

Here's an example of a landing page we built for one of our clients. It's one of the main pages of their website:

Can you spot what makes this landing page an effective one?

## Anatomy of a Good Landing Page

The following attributes make this a good landing page that yields results:

***5 Star Rating***

Without having to scroll down, the potential customer can see this is a trusted business with a five-star rating.

***Contact Number***

Putting a phone number in large text at the top of the front page increases the probability of being contacted. It also helps to express the legitimacy of the business.

***Graphics***

The media (graphic) on the landing page catches the customer's attention. In this case, our client has their logo and a "poster" of their service highlights.

***Headline***

The headline "Your Honest and Reliable Pilsen Auto Repair Specialists" tells the customer *this* auto repair shop can be trusted and is worthy of their business—and money.

### *Call to Action*

The smaller text below the headline says "Complete the form..." to let the visitor know what to do next and where to enter their information.

### *Call to Action Button*

The button is labeled: "I Need Auto Help." It speaks to the visitor's need and compels them to send their information once it has been entered in the form.

All of these components comprise an effective landing page.

### *Landing Page Process*

Due to the way the landing page is strategically structured, here's what will happen after the visitor "lands" on the page:

1. The visitor enters information about their car situation in the blank space (above the "I Need Auto Help!" button).

2. The website asks them for their name, email address, and phone number, so the business owner can reach out to them.

3. The visitor enters their contact information.

4. The contact information is emailed to the business and also stored in a mailing list (like MailChimp), so the business owner can send emails, reach out by phone, etc. in order to build a relationship with the customer.

## How to Make Riveting Landing Pages

Follow these steps to make landing pages that will produce results:

### *Brainstorm and Develop Offer Ideas*

Look at the landing page example in this chapter for inspiration, then research your competitors to find out what they are offering. Provide something different, better, more enticing, and unique to your market.

Ask yourself: What is a common problem that customers come to me for? Is there a way to give them a discounted deal?

Listen to your customers and think of your most popular services. Engage your staff members. They might have some great ideas. Figure out a way to provide something valuable to them for a sweet deal.

Remember, your *profit comes from the long-term relationships* you develop with customers. Discounts will not result in any true losses for you.

***Landing Page Format Tips***

Use your website builder to create a landing page in accordance with the example we provided. You may need to hire the help of a web designer to do this, but here are some tips:

**Front and Center**. Make sure your offer is "above the fold." Don't make customers scroll to read the offer and enter their information. Make sure your offer and contact form are visible from the get-go, similar to how a product is placed in full view on a grocery shelf.

**Website Builder Use.** If you're unsure how to build a landing page with your website builder, Google "How to make landing pages with WordPress." Replace "WordPress" with the name of your website builder program or web tool.

**Get Crucial Info!** Make sure your contact form asks for crucial information. I recommend the visitor's name, phone number, and email address at a minimum.

**Best Contact.** Connect the landing page contact form to your business email address (the one associated with MailChimp, for example). Once again, you may have to research how this is done in accordance with your website builder tool.

Pro Tip: Setup an automation to pull contact form submits automatically into MailChimp. Use a piece of software like Zapier to help you automate.

## What's Next?

You've got an offer. You're taking your market in one direction and solving customers' specific problems and pains. You also know how to put the offer out in a tangible way so you can gather your customers' contact information.

The next question is: How can you use your offer to find lots of people with car problems?

By locking in the specificity of your message and marketing, you can begin advertising to attract a large crowd of car owners. That's what I will be discussing next.

# Chapter 9: Fast-Track Profits with Pay-Per-Click Advertising

Put Your Message in Front of Ready-To-Buy Customers in Less Than 24 Hours

*"The Future of advertising is the internet"*

*-Bill Gates*

PPC (Pay-per-click) gives you the ability to launch cost-efficient ad campaigns so you can bring a flood of traffic to your site.

In this chapter, you will learn how to deploy Google's pay-per-click (or "PPC") advertising to get more customers to your website in the least amount of time possible.

That said, this chapter is not an in-depth "how-to" guide to make sure your ads succeed. It is an introduction to key concepts and terms with the hope that you will continue to research and learn on your own.

There are Google PPC specialists for a reason. The truth is, many marketers may tell you Google Ads are "easy," but these same marketers have taken a great deal of time to learn and there are tons of detailed, advanced nuances that help alleviate advertising costs. You learn these nuances through trial and error.

My goal is to help you learn how to successfully market yourself online. As long as you're dedicated to the work and research it takes to get there, the *sky will be the limit.* One thing to keep in mind is that you generally won't develop a winning ad formula immediately. It is through testing and watching to see what works that you will eventually develop a successful ad system.

Take the time to read this chapter slowly and investigate key terms. Get to know the framework of Google Ads and plan to experiment with an advertising campaign to get more visitors to your website.

## What's In It For You?

PPC (Pay-per-click) gives you the ability to launch cost-efficient ad campaigns so you can bring a flood of traffic to your site.

Rather than spending thousands of dollars on traditional advertising campaigns and getting little in return (like many large companies do), PPC allows you to bypass all the financial barriers to marketing and tap into the wealth of auto shop industry marketing opportunities immediately.

## Why PPC Ads Are Your Next Step

If you've followed the steps I've shared so far, your website now has an enticing offer and a means of gathering customer information. The next step is to open your online doors to a large number of customers who have urgent car problems.

The goal is to draw customers to your website rapidly with an automated system. The most efficient way to do that is through paid advertising.

*How Fast do PPC Ads Work?* They can work rapidly. In fact, if you set up a campaign today, you could have calls from customers coming through as soon as tomorrow morning. Of course, results like that aren't guaranteed, and you will most likely need to experiment and test a little to find the right formula.

*Do you need a lot of experience to make PPC ads work?* No. You don't have to be an advertising guru to create ads and make them work for you. You just need an organized approach to the process, testing and refinement, and the willingness to *invest* some cash.

In this chapter we will cover:

1. PPC Ad Basics.
2. How PPC Ads Work.
3. Steps to Launch a PPC Campaign.

## PPC Ad Basics

Go to Google and search "auto shop." At the top of your search results, you'll see the word "ad" written in small green letters next to the names of various auto shops. These are PPC ads and they grant the business a competitive advantage by ranking them first on the results page.

When a potential customer clicks on the ad, they are taken to whichever website or landing page has been specified in the ad campaign.

## How Do PPC Ads Work?

There are a lot of components of PPC ads, but I will cover the fundamentals here. Here are some overarching principles to keep in mind:

- PPC ads are triggered by *keyword* and *keyword phrase* searches in Google. For example, if you choose the key phrase "auto repair" for your ad, then any customer searching for that phrase in your target area will see your ad.
- The more you're willing to pay Google for your ads (the more you're willing to bid), the higher Google will prioritize your campaign. However, that's no guarantee your ad will do well. The quality of your ad and landing page matters.
- The better the quality your ad, the higher the probability that people will click and follow it to your website. Let me repeat: *Quality matters.*

Here are some key terms in the PPC domain. These will help you gain a "big picture" understanding before putting a campaign together:

### *Ad Account*

You start off by creating an ad account on Google, which is free. Within your ad account, all your campaigns will be managed.

### *Campaign*

Once you create your ad account, you create a campaign according to your budget and location.

### *Keywords*

Just like your website, all your ads have primary *keyword phrases* that customers typically use to search. For example, you may choose "oil change" as a keyword phrase for an ad. Then, whenever a customer searches for "auto repair," your ad will be displayed to them (depending on how much you've bid—more on that soon).

### ***Negative Keywords***

To ensure you don't waste money on irrelevant customer searches, you can choose to exclude keywords from your campaigns. For example, if you are targeting customers who are seeking only shop services, you might want to exclude the phrase "car parts."

You can find general negative keyword lists to add to your campaigns online. An example of a negative keyword list would be keywords that would be associated with job hunting like "hire", "job" and "jobs". For example, someone might search "auto repair jobs". *Think about this intuitively*, someone who's searching this phrase wouldn't be your ideal customer, they're looking for a job, not to get their car repaired. So, with the inclusion of your negative keyword list for job searchers, your ad would never even display for this individual.

Now I know what you're thinking, why does this matter if I'm paying per click? *Google grades your ad based on its quality*, the fewer clicks it receives per

1,000 views, the lower the quality score. Essentially Google is punishing you for showing your ad to the wrong searchers (remember that Google wants to keep its searchers happy too). As a result, Google will raise your cost per click and that in turn makes everything else more expensive which generally leads to a failed campaign. More on this in a bit.

### *Ad Groups*

Ad Groups provide a powerful way to "super target" your customers by grouping your ads by themes.

For example, if you want to attract customers who search for "auto repair" and related keywords, such as "automobile repair," you can dedicate an Ad Group to those permutations. If, on the other hand, you want to target customers searching for "oil change" and related keywords, you can create another Ad Group for that purpose.

### *Bidding (Manual or Automated)*

You won't be the only auto shop owner using PPC and competing with other shops to appear at the top of Google search results. Therefore, you will need to specify the maximum amount you are willing to "pay per click."

Important note: If you don't hire someone like me to manually manage your ads, I recommend choosing "automated bidding," for your preferred bidding method—unless you're willing to research and learn the science of ad bidding.

### *Ad Content & Copy*

Ad content & copy refers to the words your potential customers read when they find your ad on Google. Your ad content should mention the features of your offer, how your offer benefits the customer, and a call-to-action (similar to the structure of your landing page).

### *Impressions*

Once you launch your ads, Google tracks the number of "Impressions" it serves. Impressions are the number of times Google shows your ads to people—regardless of whether they click on it or not. "Clicks" refer to the number of times potential customers click on your ad.

### *Cost per click (CPC)*

This is the amount you pay Google every time a customer clicks on your ad. This cost is based on a few variables, including competition and the quality of your ad.

### *Clickthrough Rate (CTR)*

Google calculates this rate to help determine your Quality Score. It is the number of clicks divided by the number of impressions. So, if you have 100 impressions and 2 clicks, your CTR would be 2%.

### *Quality Score*

The quality score is Google's way of assessing the overall value and importance of your ad in the market. It is calculated based on several variables including:

- **Previous Google Ads Performance.** Data from your past efforts affect the quality score of your current ads.

- **CTR.** Your clickthrough rate contributes to the final quality score of your ad.
- **Keyword Relevance.** If the keywords within an Ad Group are related to one another, you'll achieve better keyword relevance.
- **Landing Page Quality.** When your landing page is coherent and gives your visitors a quality experience, your ad quality score will go up.

Most importantly, the higher your landing page quality score, the lower your ads cost.

***Optimization***

Once you launch the campaign, you should assess how it is performing and make necessary tweaks to maximize revenue. This process is known as "optimization."

## Launch a PPC Campaign

Take the following steps to launch a PPC campaign:

1. **Create** a Google Ads account.

2. **Create** an Ad Campaign based on a daily budget and location. For example, maybe you want to target car owners in Rockford Illinois and spend a maximum of $10 a day (it's a good idea to start small). Note: Campaign settings also include options about your target audience and ad extensions (which I will explain soon).

3. **Create** an Ad Group within your campaign based on a "keyword family," meaning keywords that are specific and similar. Example: Ad Group Name: Oil Change. Keywords: oil change, oil filter, tune-up, etc.

**4.** **Create ads** within your ad groups that speak to each keyword in the keyword family. For example, if your Ad Group has three keywords similar to "auto repair," then you may have three ads, each targeted toward the individual keywords.

5. **Write** headlines and content for each ad.

6. **Connect** your ads to landing pages (or any target page) within your site.

7. **Launch** campaign, monitor the results, make any necessary changes.

There are of course many refining details in each of these steps, but at any rate, they comprise the main "campaign cycle" steps.

Pro Tip: Create multiple landing pages, one for each keyword or ad group depending on how granular you want to get. This segregation will boost your conversion rates because each searcher sees a closer message match between their search and the landing page they view.

### *Research With Spyfu*

If you're just beginning with Google Ads, finding the right keywords for your ads can be a grueling process.

*Spyfu* makes the process easy. Alternatively hire a freelancer to get this done for you.

Once you purchase the service, you can plug in your competitor's website URL's and the Spyfu website will provide recommended keywords for your PPC campaigns.

*Spyfu* costs around $40 a month, but it's well worth the price and will save you hours—and even months—of time figuring out the best keywords. Follow these steps to get Spyfu:

1. **Go** to spyfu.com.

2. **Choose** the annual or monthly plan.

3. **Get to know** the interface.

4. **Go** to Google and **search** for auto shops in your area. These are your competitors. For example, if you are in Rockford, Illinois, you could search for "auto shop Rockford, IL."

5. **Check** the top of the search results for green-colored ad links.

6. **Right-click** on an ad link and select "Copy link."

7. **Paste** the address in a Word document or any other word processor. You're saving the web address (URL) of your competitor for later.

8. **Repeat** the copy/paste process with one or two more shops in the search results. Find as many competitors as you want.

9. The more data you have, the better.

10. **Analyze** your competitors with *Spyfu* (refer to their support for specific steps).

Write down all the recommended keywords Spyfu lists and save them for later.

Spyfu will also show how long your competitors' ads have been running. Chances are, if an ad has been running for a year it's probably a profitable ad. Who in their right mind would keep a losing ad up for a year?

### *Get to Know Google Ads.*

As with other steps in previous chapters, it would be impossible to teach you how to use Google Ads within one short marketing book. That said, Google has a pretty intuitive support system.

If you haven't created a Google Ads account yet, you can do so here:

https://ads.google.com/intl/en_us/lp/coupons/.

Then follow these steps:

1. **Log into** your Ads account.

2. **Click** "help" the "help" button. Look to the top right: it is a question mark in a circle.

3. **Select** "guided steps."

4. **Read** each "chapter" of the guided tutorials. Set aside an hour or two a night to work through them. Make sure you take breaks every so often; there's a lot of information to digest.

It's important to note that Google Ads success is not guaranteed, especially for your first campaign.

Think of yourself as a scientist, experimenting until you find the perfect advertising formula for your shop. This is how all successful campaigns begin. There's no perfect starting point.

It may be difficult to accept that you may lose cash in the process of finding what works. In fact, many business owners have lost thousands of dollars by misusing Google Ads, which is why they often hire someone to take care of it for them.

However, if your priority is to teach yourself, and you are willing to dedicate a few months of your time, it may be worth it. It really depends on your priorities.

In the end, the investment of time and money is worthy if you find a winning advertisement that boosts profits and creates long-term customers. Think about how much one of your returning customers may pay you in the lifetime of their vehicle. I'd estimate your average customer value to be somewhere between $2,000-$5,000.

Now multiply that figure by three, four, five, or ten. Aren't those the kinds of returns you're ultimately after?

Here's the great news. Once you find a winning advertisement, you can put the campaign on autopilot and accrue high-value leads non-stop and avoid spending large amounts of money on traditional advertising.

## The Six Big PPC Mistakes

Studies show most failed campaigns make mistakes that can be placed into one of six categories: Tracking, Targeting, Messaging, Bidding, Creativity, and/or Funnel Structure.

I've provided some basic examples of mistakes here, but take time to research each of these factors as you get to know the Google Ads interface.

### *Mistake #1: Tracking*

Failing to track important details about the campaign and misunderstanding how metrics work. Even if you've spent hours creating and launching a campaign, it's not simply a matter of waiting for leads to appear.

It's important to track what time of day most of your leads arrive, which keywords are most profitable, and how many leads who click on your ad opt into the landing page on your site.

Tools like Wordstream's "Ads Performance Grader" (wordstream.com) automatically generate reports to let you know how your campaign is performing, why it may be failing, and what can be done to improve your results.

Other tracking mistakes include failing to track conversions accurately. If you aren't tracking "conversions" the right way, then you won't know how many visitors are turning into paying customers. Why? Because many people who click on your ad may not opt in to your website offer.

The key is to measure how many people fill out a form on your landing page, which is closer to a sale than a mere click on your ad. Google has tracking options for that very purpose so make sure you use them.

Furthermore, if you have customers bring in a coupon from an advertisement, you can track how many of them have purchased from a campaign. This is an important metric to accurately judge the ROI (return on investment) of your campaign.

For best results, develop a system and schedule your time to put ads out, check the performance of the campaign, and make modifications as needed.

If you stick to the process of testing, refining, and researching your PPC stats, you will eventually make your campaign work for you.

Finding a winning advertisement from scratch without experience is a process of elimination in which you continue to rule out what doesn't work until the winner is left standing. So create multiple ads and split test them against each other to see which ads perform the best.

That said, I can't say it enough: Prepare to sacrifice a good amount of time and cash if you go the DIY route.

### *Mistake #2: Targeting/Keywords*

A common mistake is making keywords too broad. Remember the previous chapter about offers? Specificity is important for revenue and profit.

The more specific your keywords, the better your ads will perform, as long as your customers are searching for them (Spyfu can provide profitable keywords in this respect).

Taking advantage of the Ad Groups feature is *critical* for avoiding targeting mistakes. By using multiple Ad Groups, you can target many different keyword families. Without this feature, you will miss out on other Google searches potential customers are making.

For example, if you want to target "oil change" and "auto repair," you can create two separate Ad Groups for each phrase. Within those keyword phrases, you can create ads for specific permutations.

For example, in the Ad Group for "oil change," you could run an ad targeted towards "cheap oil change." Then you could run another ad for "oil changes."

In the ad group for "auto repair," you could run an ad targeted toward "automotive repair" and another toward "vehicle repair." In the end you will have created ads tailored to your customers' specific problems.

Bear in mind, these are just examples for illustration, and I don't recommend applying them verbatim in your campaign.

If you neglect Ad Groups, then you're obligated to put multiple diverse keywords in one group. This compromises the quality of your ad, which will increase your costs.

### *Mistake #3: Messaging*

Contrary to popular belief, the lifeblood of your PPC campaign is not limited to great keywords, but also consistent messaging. You must use similar keywords in your Ad Groups and then include those same keywords in your ad content. Also, make sure your ad content wording matches your landing page wording. The goal is to share one, unified message throughout your whole online marketing system.

Since you've begun learning how to construct a decent landing page, you're already ahead of the curve in this respect. Part of Google's ad ranking system looks at what your customers experience once they click on your ad and visit your website. In the end, how your ad performs depends on the entire structure of your sales funnel.

### *Mistake #4: Bidding*

Unless you understand the math behind bidding, I highly recommend automating the process (Google has an option for that). There are tons of other bidding options you can choose from, which may work better than automation in the long term, but only if you understand how those bidding operations work.

### *Mistake #5: Creative/Copywriting*

If your ad text is written in a boring way or is devoid of psychological triggers that influence your customers to click, then your entire campaign can flop, even with everything else set correctly.

Write compelling headlines and ad content that piques your reader's curiosity and suggests a quick and easy solution to their problem. There are tons of "writing formulas" on the web from top-notch copywriters. Use them and they'll work perfectly.

### *Mistake #6: Funnel Structure*

This was addressed in previous chapters, but if you don't take your visitors to a compelling landing page and opportunity, gather their contact information, and stay in touch with them via email or phone after they opt-in, then you may be burning cash.

The point of advertising isn't to make your company known or visible on the web; it is to catch the attention of your market, get in contact with them, dialogue with them long enough to build a relationship and build their trust so they have a reason to buy from you.

Your PPC advertisement is the forefront of a sales funnel, a set of steps that help your customer feel at home and assures them you truly care about their problem.

## Other PPC Best Practices

### *Location Specificity*

When you create a campaign, your ads can be location-specific. Since most customers won't travel very far to get their car serviced, I recommend setting your ad "radius" within 1-2 miles in a major city. For rural shops, expand the radius further. By doing this, you'll be focusing on a target market.

### *Ad Extensions*

Ad Extensions allow you to add extra lines of text or information that are known to increase conversion rates. Use these as much as needed. For example, you can add your hours and location to your ad, links to multiple pages of your site (not recommended for a landing page campaign) and include additional headlines with important information about your offer. These are highly recommended.

If you end up using the "call" extension, which gives your customers the ability to call you from the ad, make sure you only schedule it to run during your business hours.

***Retargeting***

You can set up a tracking system that shows your ads multiple times to previous website visitors when they navigate to sites other than your own. Retargeting ads are *powerful and cheap.*

Here's how it works. When the visitor lands on your page, Google "tracks" them using a "cookie," then places your ad in front of them repeatedly wherever they go—including social media sites like Facebook.

As an advertiser, it may be easy to assume this could be annoying and invasive to the customer, but it is a part of the internet now and retargeting extends the lifetime value of your campaign. More on retargeting in Chapter 10, which covers Facebook Advertising.

Once you find success with a PPC campaign on Google Ads, you can copy your exact campaign over to Microsoft Advertising (formerly Bing Ads). The advantage of Microsoft Ads is a lower cost per click. Also, the audience tends to be a bit less tech-savvy than people that use Google and generally tend to be a bit older.

## What's Next?

So now you've learned how to place your message in front of potential customers with very high search intent. Reach out to me if you have questions that aren't covered in this book on PPC. In the next chapter we'll discuss advertising on Facebook, similar concepts, but a whole different world.

# Chapter 10: Reach More Customers with Facebook Ads

Harness Facebook's Algorithm to Get Your Message in Front of the Right Audience

---

*"Many a small thing has been made large by advertisimg"*

*-Mark Twain*

---

Facebook has the largest gathering of people in the world. That creates a major opportunity for advertisers who know how to use it.

Facebook is an *incredibly powerful* advertising tool for the average auto shop since it allows them to hyper-target local audiences by age, gender, interests, etc. As a result, I classify it as a much more powerful tool than most PPC options if done correctly.

In the last chapter we went over PPC on Google Ads. In this chapter I will teach you how to

1. Leverage the *incredible reach* of Facebook to attract more customers to your website.

2. Create *powerful retargeting* ads that draw interested buyers back to you.

3. Force your ads to perform by split testing

## What's In It For You?

Facebook ads have a much lower cost per click. If you're a Facebook user, think about why you go on there. To connect with family and friends, to consume news, learn about things in groups and watch videos you find entertaining. As a result, in general Facebook audience has a *lower intent* than people searching on Google.

Facebook's demographics are much more detailed; you can target and segregate audiences with a great level of flexibility. People searching Google are looking for *something now*, which Google capitalizes on and charges a much higher cost per click. As a result, Facebook ads can be much more profitable if done right because of the much lower cost per click.

## Why Facebook Ads Are Your Next Step

Google is the most popular search engine in the world and therefore your website must be wired to it to capitalize on searchers. However, Google isn't the only place your customers hang out. Facebook is just as popular and, as I said at the beginning, it's critically important you are "present" wherever your potential customers are. Connecting your website with Google and Facebook creates a powerful *profit triangle* you can't afford to miss.

## Creating a Facebook Campaign

Our main goal is to drive traffic from local customers as cheaply as possible. For this purpose, when you create your Facebook campaign, choose "traffic" as the objective. Follow these tips for best results.

### *Target Your audience*

Keep it tight, target your audience to within 1-2 miles of your shop if in a highly-populated area. If you're in a more rural area, expand your audience radius.

### *Watch Your Targeting*

As far as targeting for gender, typically a good place to start is by running ads wide open to every person in the targeted radius around your shop. From there you can see who's clicking on your ads. You might notice that your ad is being clicked on by mainly men. Women are clicking but at a much higher cost per click. In that case, if you cut out women entirely, you can lower your cost per click and as a result be more efficient with your ad spend.

### *Add in Interest Targeting*

If you're a specialty shop you can target based on demographics like income or interests. Say for example, you're running a shop that only repairs BMW's you would want to interest target people who like Bayerische Motoren Werke. You can also target the top 10% of income in a zip code as BMW drivers are generally *more affluent* than Toyota drivers for example. Didn't I say Facebook Ads are *powerful*?

Facebook's algorithm works really well, so don't specify too many interests, Most people need to visit a shop a couple of times a year so you'll be catering to a broader audience.

A note from the author

I've placed you on the right path, however, targeting is just too difficult to write about in any certainty, so each situation needs to be evaluated on its own merits. Therefore, if you have specific questions on targeting, email me at and I'll point you in the right direction.

jonathan@socialleafmarketing.com.

### *Set a Budget*

I recommend you start small. Start at $5 to $10 per day and see what works in your area. You can analyze your ad performance by "split testing" (more on split testing later in this chapter).

As you increase your budget, Facebook's algorithm gathers data on what types of people are responding best to your ads. This allows your ad to get more efficient as you spend more money. Think of it as Facebook's way of thanking you for spending money with them.

### *Add Your Landing Pages*

Remember when we talked about landing pages in chapter 8? The same concept applies to Facebook ads.

The goal is to send customers to a landing page that *compels* them to take a specific action—whether the action is to download a coupon or signup for your monthly newsletter.

### *Choose the Right Ad Format*

From what I've seen in the advertising space for auto shops, video is often more effective than pictures, but this varies based on location and demographics. Try both a video ad and picture ad and split test them against each other. This brings us to the next point: ad optimization.

### *Optimizing Ads*

Similar to Google PPC Ads, as a general rule, you won't strike gold immediately when creating and running a Facebook campaign. Facebook has an algorithm that will help make your ad more efficient as it sees more data, but the initial setup mostly rests on your inputs. Facebook ads need to be constantly refined and tested to achieve a higher return on investment.

How do you know if you're succeeding? You measure cost per conversion for each ad. A conversion is when a customer takes a specific action like downloading a coupon. Facebook can track this using "Pixel" and allow you to see what ads/placements etc. are driving conversions at the lowest cost.

### ***Split Testing***

*Think about it this way*

If Facebook ads were easy, everyone would be running them, ad agencies wouldn't exist. You need a way to guarantee that your ad will *travel to profit* and split testing is the way to allow that to happen.

One of the most important ad optimization pieces to focus on is the "split test." Split testing is like putting a car on a dyno with certain settings and then rerunning with different settings to see which results in *more horsepower.*

For example, if you create an ad for new customers showcasing a coupon that offers $50 off $300 or more in repairs, you can duplicate that ad, change the title, then run the two ads against each other to see which one gets more conversions. You can test all pieces of the ad including the picture, copy (copy refers to ad text), etc. The possibilities are *endless.*

### ***Display Options***

There are different places you can display your ads on Facebook. As a general rule, the most *profitable space*—but also expensive—is right on the newsfeed.

Picture yourself scrolling down your Facebook newsfeed when all of the sudden you see an ad amongst your other posts. Hard to miss. As a general rule, news feed ads are the safest and most profitable option.

But Facebook also offers other areas to advertise, such as Messenger. Sometimes an ad displayed on a less expensive location like Messenger can be *insanely profitable.* But to keep things safe, we typically start with feed placements on Facebook or Instagram timelines.

Of course, if you track ads closely, you will see how different placements perform. For example, one auto shop might notice they've spent 10% of their budget in Messenger placements with zero conversions. This drives up cost per conversion for the other placements, so that shop owner would want to cancel the Messenger ads.

### *Watch Your Demographics*

Take a look at who's driving conversions. You may find that ad conversions are 90% men while half of your ad spend is on women. If you target only males on Facebook, you'll probably notice that your cost per conversion suddenly drops in half. Now you're only spending $30 per repair order rather than $55, and your money's going a lot further.

### *Harness Facebook Retargeting*

Retargeting gives you the power to target Facebook users (while they are on Facebook) who have: previously *taken action* on your website, called you recently from your website, or have seen or interacted with one of your advertisements.

Here's an example. A prospective customer named James clicks on your website after finding you on Google (this is called an "organic" search), but then gets distracted and closes your website and goes about his day. You can create a special advertisement that James sees while he is on Facebook. That ad will often influence him to click and come back to your website… or call or email you. Because James is already familiar with you, he's a *lot more likely* to click than a cold audience.

Facebook retargeting ads are generally very cheap and displayed to a small audience, so there is no reason not to run them. They also offer *super-high conversion rates* because they are being shown only to people who are already considering your shop.

So how do you know if people are clicking your Facebook retargeting ads and coming to your website? Great question. That's where Facebook's "Pixel" tracking code comes in.

### *Using the Magical Facebook Pixel*

Facebook's "Facebook Pixel" is a funny name to describe a grouping of code Facebook wrote to put on your website and help you track the effectiveness of your Facebook ads. The code collects data and tracks conversions from Facebook ads, helps optimize ads and build targeted audiences for future ads, and remarkets to people who have already taken some kind of *action* on your website.

There are a bunch of ways to install the Pixel on your website that vary based on what you've used to build that website. That said, once your Pixel is installed, I'd suggest using the chrome add-on called "Pixel Tracker" to ensure the Pixel is installed on your website correctly. If you have specific questions on installing the Pixel, contact me directly and I'll help you get setup: jonathan@socialleafmarketing.com.

Great, so now we've got your Pixel all installed on your website, it will talk to Facebook and track what actions were taken on your website, and from those actions you can *refine* your retargeting strategy.

## Retargeting Best Practices

Follow all these best practices to build a *killer retargeting campaign.*

### *Select "Reach"*

When setting up a retargeting campaign on Facebook, set your marketing objective as "Reach." This ensures your ad is shown to as many people as possible and as often as possible.

*Gather a big enough audience size*

A problem that I see a lot when people are retargeting is that their audience is not big enough. If your audience is below 100, Facebook won't run retargeting ads to them. An example of an audience would be customers that visited your Instagram page within the past 30 days. Let's talk about how to *define* your custom retargeting audience.

### *Define a Custom Audience*

When Facebook prompts you to select an audience, choose a custom audience. With a custom audience you can *narrow your audience down greatly*. For example, you could target people who like your images on Facebook or Instagram. You could also target people who have visited your website within the past 30 days.

### *Choose a Reasonable Ad Frequency*

You can choose to display the retargeting ad, e.g., seven times over the next seven days. Or you could create another advertisement that shows seven times over seven days with a different creative. By "creative" I mean how the ad looks and sounds in comparison to the other ad. Consumers often get ad fatigue if they're shown the same ad more than five times, so vary your ad creative to reduce fatigue.

Facebook ads can also be *powerful* when shown locally to first-time customers. There are a couple of guidelines that you'll want to follow to make sure that you get started with a profitable ad campaign. The tips I've shared will help you start with a solid *platform of profitability*.

## What's Next?

Just as a car is bound to run into problems once it starts up and takes on some wear and tear, there will also be opportunities to optimize and fix your online marketing vehicle as customers interact with it, especially once your first campaign is up and running. You can only do that when you are able to properly diagnose potential problems in your system by using *analytics.*

In the next chapter, you'll learn how to implement analytics to ensure *no money falls through the cracks of your entire system.*

# Part 3: Hold the Vehicle Together and Travel to Success Multiply Your Profit

# Chapter 11: Run Diagnostic Tests and Study Analytics

Diagnose Problems, Fix, Refine, and Optimize Your System

*"It doesn't matter whether you are pursuing success in business, sports, the arts, or life in general: The bridge between wishing and accomplishing is discipline."*

*-Harvey Mackay*

Don't wait to set up tracking systems, or you could be wasting a lot of money on your marketing campaigns without knowing it.

## What's In It For You?

Much like a diagnostics test with vehicles, analytics give you the ability to track the "health" of your marketing efforts.

Analytics allow you to easily understand exactly what your potential customers are doing on your website, how they are responding to your ads, and where they are on their *journey* to your auto-shop doorstep. So to be clear there are many types of analytics, but in this chapter we're talking about watching search and paid traffic to your website.

*The more you track, the more you will be able to optimize your efforts* and increase your return on investment. When you optimize your efforts, your vehicle runs better so you can travel further to profit.

By the end of this chapter, you will know how to use online analytics to track the "health" of your marketing efforts. And what this means for you is greater visibility and control over your marketing.

## Why Analytics Are Your Next Step

You shouldn't wait to set up tracking systems, or else you could be *wasting a lot of money* on your marketing campaigns without knowing it.

Just because you get three customers in a week does not mean there aren't three others who were turned off by your website, for example.

In such a case, the probability of your success is minimized because of statistics you choose to ignore by neglecting the measurable side of marketing.

Treat analytics like diagnostic tests. It's nearly impossible to accurately identify the causes of your hidden problems unless you implement metrics for good judgment.

In this chapter I will cover:

1. The basics of Analytics.
2. How Analytics Work.
3. Setting Up Analytics.

## Basics of Analytics

Analytics usually come in the form of graphs and other data on a panel to show you how well your online strategy is performing.

There are analytic tools for most major online platforms, including Google and social media, but what they all have in common are the statistics they provide by leveraging insights on customer activity and interactions with your website(s).

## How Analytics Work

Analytics are similar to placing a GPS tracker on a car. In the case of websites, you place "code" on your website, which gathers all the relevant analytical data and displays it in a "dashboard" on your web browser. Here are some essential components to get familiar with:

### *The Analytics Tag*

To gather data from your website, Google provides you with a "tag" to copy and paste into your website's source code. Where you place the tag depends on what tool you're using to manage your website, so it takes some research on your part to apply it.

### *Reports*

There are generally traffic, activity, and conversion reports. Once Google transfers the data from your website into your Analytics account, it provides reports about the traffic to your site, activity on the pages, and how many of your customers have opted into your landing page forms.

## Setting Up Analytics

1. **Go** to https://analytics.google.com and create a new Google Analytics account.

2. **Create** a new "Property" for your Website. "Property" is just a fancy name for telling Google Analytics what website you want to track.

3. **Click** on the Admin button in the left pane of the Analytics panel (with the gear icon).

4. **Click** on "Create Property" in the property column.

5. **Follow** the instructions and enter the URL of your website so Google knows which site to track.

6. **Click** Create to finish the process.

7. **Click** on the Admin button again. In the property column, make sure your website is selected

in the dropdown menu (this will be the case if you only have one property).

8. **Click** on Tracking Info.

9. **Click** on Tracking Code.

10. **Copy** the script onto your clipboard (under the heading Global Site Tag).

***Integrate Analytics with Your Website***

Research to find out how to integrate analytics with your website and builder. If you use WordPress, here's how to do it:

1. **Copy** the Analytics tag to your clipboard (see the previous step).

2. **Log** into your account.

3. **Click** Appearance on the left side of the dashboard, then click Editor.

4. **Click** on the header.php file under the Templates section.

5. **Paste** the code before the closing *</header>* tag.

6. **Click** on *Update File.*

### *Test Your Analytics*

1. **Visit** your own website once.

2. **Log** into your Analytics Account.

3. **Click** on Admin.

4. **Click** Reports in the left column.

5. **Click** on Real-Time.

6. **Click** the "X" on the guide that fills up the window. If your Analytics tag is implemented correctly, your website visit should be registered in the data.

Now, spend some time getting to know the Analytics interface, especially the different kinds of Reports you can view.

### *What to do with all the data and reports?*

As you get to know the Analytics interface, you'll notice what seems to be an insurmountable quantity of data and numbers to deal with.

Every metric you track will help you understand how, where, and when your customers interact with your business online. When you understand how your audience interacts and moves around, then you can shadow them with the rhythm of your marketing.

There are *three fundamental reports* to monitor when you start off:

**Audience Behavior Reports.** Allow you to assess how many new visitors are showing up, and how many are returning.

**The Landing Pages Report.** Identifies where on your site most visitors congregate, depart, etc.

**Conversion Reports.** Tracks how many visitors opt-in to your landing page form (if you have one).

If you want to track landing page metrics, you'll have to take a few steps:

1. **Create** a "Thank You" page a visitor is taken to once they submit their information from your landing page. On the Thank You page, include a friendly message, such as, "Thanks for your inquiry!

We'll get back to you within one business day." (Be specific, and follow through as promised!)

2. **Write down** the tail end of your landing page URL. For example, if your landing page URL is www.fixmycarz.com/landingpage.html than the tail is "/landingpage.html." Copy everything after ".com."

3. **Create** a Goal in Google Analytics.

a. **Click** on Admin.

b. **Find** the Goals button under the View column to the right and click on it.

c. **Click** on the New Goal button.

4. **Select** Sign Up in the settings under the Engagement heading near the bottom. Then click on Continue.

5. **Name** your goal anything you like, then click on Continue.

6. **Select** "Destination" as the Type, then click on Continue.

7. **Select** "Begins with" from the dropdown menu under Goal Details

8. **Paste** the tail end of your landing page address in the space next to "Begins with." **Leave** Value and Funnel in the Off position

9. **Click** Save.

If done correctly, your landing page activity is now being tracked and can be examined via the Conversions Report.

There are numerous other reports which can be useful, depending on the nuances of your marketing strategy. However, as a business owner, your biggest priority ought to be making sure more people are visiting your pages, understanding where they are going, and how many are opting in (if you have a landing page form set up).

Bear in mind, opt-in rates are not indicative of how much money you're making from your website visitors. Only a certain percentage of people opting in will end up buying a service.

Keep an eye on your bounce rate, when a customer bounces that means they went on to your website, sees something that they didn't like and then immediately clicked back or closed out the website. An average bounce rate that we see in the auto shop industry is anywhere from 41%-55%. If your bounce rate is 80% you might have a problem with your message, or you might be ranking for the wrong keywords.

## What's Next?

At this point, your entire foundational marketing vehicle is built. Congrats! With analytics, you're measuring potential problems and making sure every component runs efficiently. In other words, you can take your customers on a joy ride from start to finish.

But how will you make sure to call each of them back once they pick up the phone and dial your shop? How can you *easily and automatically capitalize on every opportunity* with customers who are trying to reach you through your campaigns? You'll learn how in the next chapter.

# Chapter 12: Improve Your Marketing Mileage With Call Tracking

*"Opportunities are like sunrises. If you wait too long, you miss them."*

*-William Arthur Ward*

If you run a busy shop, just one forgotten or missed call can mean a few thousand dollars burned. It's no different than burning oil, really.

**What's In It For You?**

If you run a shop that gets really busy, just one forgotten missed call can mean a few thousand dollars burned. It's no different than burning oil, really.

By implementing call tracking, you'll never miss a customer who calls you in response to your advertisements. In turn, this will increase the *efficiency of your cash flow*.

## Why Call Tracking Is Your Next Step

The final step in a solid digital marketing strategy is to integrate everything you've created electronically with your team inside the shop walls and merging your systems with your people.

In other words, to maximize the results of all the previous steps in this book, automation of the customer tracking process seals the deal. The more organized you are, the quicker you can call your customers back, which means more money in your pocket.

In this chapter you'll learn *everything* you need to know to ensure you never miss a customer who calls you in response to your advertisements. In turn, your ROI and cash flow will increase.

## How Call Tracking Works

Similar to analytics, call tracking involves pasting a "snippet" or "tag" into the code of your campaign or website, which will enable you to track why customers called you and how.

For example, if you want to call back customers who traveled to your website from a specific keyword in Google, you can do that. If you want to call back customers who interacted with your landing page, you can do that as well.

***The Snippet***

Similar to the Tag from Google Analytics, the snippet is pasted on a landing page of your website, then calls made from the page can be tracked.

***Tracking (Source or Keyword)***

You can either track calls according to where the snippet was placed (source), or you can categorize calls based on the keyword your customer searched for.

In other words, with keyword tracking, you can store calls made by customers who searched for "auto repair" or "auto shops."

This can be helpful when you want to optimize campaigns and figure out what specifically made your customer pick up the phone to dial your number.

***Recommended Call Tracker***

We recommend **Callrail** (callrail.com) to all our clients. Their features are versatile, and the customer support is tremendous. Once you purchase the service, you can follow along with the instructions and integrate it with your strategy

Pro Tip: Callrail allows you to see if your front desk is calling customers back. You can also listen in and hear how your front desk is handling calls. Of course be sure to check if your state is a one party consent state for voice recording.

## Next Steps

It's time to look at all we've covered and discussed. On the next few pages, you'll find an overview of the entire puzzle put together, including all the material from each chapter combined into one big picture.

# Conclusion

Your Marketing Vehicle. Frame, Body, and All.

---

*"Coming together is a beginning,
staying together is progress, and
working together is success. If you
think you can do a thing or think you
can't do a thing, you're right..."*

*-Henry Ford*

---

In this chapter we will firm up everything this book has covered.

To see the entire marketing vehicle you've built in action, let's return to our fictional character Ralph and see what happens when your marketing vehicle is firing on all cylinders.

After Ralph's car breaks down, he searches Google for "auto repair" in his area.

Because you have a Google My Business Page set up and your business is indexed on Google Maps, Ralph sees your shop right away. The five-star reviews assure him you're most likely not a scam. (Chapters 1-3)

Additionally, Ralph notices an ad running for your shop at the top of the page. Between your ad and Google Maps entry, the repeated occurrence of your business name on the front page grabs his attention. (Chapter 9)

Ralph visits your website, which is in clear alignment with his primary search phrases (Chapter 4). Your home page looks really simple and clean with staff photos, testimonials, location/contact information, and clear shop descriptions, thus increasing your credibility (Chapter 6).

Next, Ralph clicks on the phone number link on your page and calls you. Lucky for him (and you), you happen to pick up.

Now you're talking to Ralph about his situation and diagnosing potential issues based on the symptoms he's describing.

Because of Ralph's experience online with Google prior to picking up the phone, your conversation with him seals the deal—he trusts you and calls to have his car towed to your shop.

*And that's just the beginning...*

Thanks to your analytical measures, you're now able to track how Ralph found you and which keywords he searched prior to picking up the phone (Chapters 10-11). Now you can refine your marketing efforts and use similar keywords to attract more customers just like Ralph.

While Ralph waits for the tow truck, he gets bored, so he opts in for the discounted offer coupon for an oil change on your front page. He checks his email and receives the coupon (Chapters 7 and 8).

Now, you're able to build a relationship with Ralph via email once his car is fixed. You have generated a new, long term high-value opportunity from just one customer. (Chapter 5)

People like Ralph aren't rare, so neither are powerful and profitable opportunities.

And it's all because you *welcomed Ralph into your world* through an online marketing vehicle.

There you have it, friend: Your online marketing blueprint-roadmap hybrid. I gave you a highway, lit up the streets, and the signs I've provided are sure to give you direction if you follow them as many of our other clients have.

## You Learned to Build a Marketing Vehicle from Scratch. Now What?

One marketing book cannot give you all the answers, but this one certainly will suffice to lay a solid foundation to continue building on your knowledge.

As for me, I've been inspired by the efforts of many auto shop owners, especially those who desire to genuinely grow their business and become known as high-quality technicians who supersede the shady reputations of their competitors.

If that describes you, I'm glad you picked up a copy of this book and hope you will share it with others. When one of us succeeds, we all succeed.

That said, if you are eager for a fast-track to success, go ahead and reach out to me at:

**jonathan@socialleafmarketing.com**.

We can connect and discuss a potential partnership. We do have a full service done for you marketing agency that focuses specifically on the auto shop industry.

And if you've finished this entire book, I'd like to offer you something special. I call it a strategy session, where I take a deep dive and point out the areas of your marketing that if fixed can have the biggest impact on your shop's revenue. You're getting years of trial and error condensed down into 30 minutes of complimentary consulting with no pressure to partner.

Go to:

**calendly.com/socialleafgrowth**

to take advantage of this offer and use promo code Book2020.

You can also check out our website at:

**socialleafmarketing.com/automotive**

Otherwise, safe travels, and enjoy your journey!

Made in the USA
Monee, IL
09 November 2020

47056258R00132